Research on Intercultural Foreign Language Teaching Practice

跨文化外语教学实践研究

吕宁 著

中国纺织出版社有限公司

图书在版编目（CIP）数据

跨文化外语教学实践研究 = Research on Intercultural Foreign Language Teaching Practice / 吕宁著 . --北京 ：中国纺织出版社有限公司，2023.8
　ISBN 978-7-5229-0764-2

　Ⅰ. ①跨… Ⅱ. ①吕… Ⅲ. ①英语—外语教学—教学研究 Ⅳ. ①H319.3

中国国家版本馆 CIP 数据核字（2023）第 129759 号

KUA WENHUA WAIYU JIAOXUE SHIJIAN YANJIU

责任编辑：朱利锋　 责任校对：高　涵　 责任印制：王艳丽

中国纺织出版社有限公司出版发行
地址：北京市朝阳区百子湾东里 A407 号楼　邮政编码：100124
销售电话：010—67004422　传真：010—87155801
http://www.c-textilep.com
中国纺织出版社天猫旗舰店
官方微博 http://weibo.com/2119887771
天津千鹤文化传播有限公司印刷　各地新华书店经销
2023 年 8 月第 1 版第 1 次印刷
开本：710×1000　1/16　印张：7.5
字数：100 千字　定价：78.00 元

前　言

　　1964 年，加拿大传播学学者马歇尔·麦克卢汉创造了著名的"地球村"一词，他预见世界将发展成为一个小村庄（McLuhan，1964）。根据他的观点，使世界变小的并不是高度发达的媒体技术，而是人类的沟通方式。今天，麦克卢汉的预言正在变成现实。不同国家和不同文化之间的交流得到了大规模的普及。跨文化活动，如跨文化合作、跨文化援助、跨文化交流、跨国公司、国际商业、跨文化婚姻、人际沟通，一直是我们生活中不可或缺的一部分。一切都正在变得越来越国际化和跨文化。就像陈国明（2005）所说："全球化已经突破了人类社会空间、时间、文化假设，以及范畴、结构和功能的界限。"这种挑战使得跨文化交际能力成为招聘市场上人才的关键构成要素，尤其是那些精通一门或多门外语并能流利交流的人才变得非常抢手。今天，如果我们研究一下各种招聘广告，很容易发现跨文化交际能力（ICC）在就业市场上是一种需求度很高的素质。科布林（1984）调查了 217 家美国的跨国公司，发现跨文化交流能力（用他的话来说是"国际专业能力"）对许多需要进行国际性交流的公司来说非常重要，对这些员工的晋升也同样非常有利。高等学校外语专业教学指导委员会面向涉及各部委、国有企业、外贸公司和教育等领域的用人单位做了一项调查。结果显示，雇主对外语专业毕业生的需求已经降到了 0.66%，而且受访雇主希望外语专业的学生能够拓宽他们的知识面。因此，外语专业的学生在就业市场正在失去他们的优势。

　　同时，《高等学校英语专业英语教学大纲》（2000）列出了 21 世纪外语人才应具备的五种素质（详见第三章）：扎实的语言基础、广泛的知识面、一定的专业知识、较高的能力和较好的素质。它们听起来很笼统，然而，在《高等学校英语专业英语教学大纲》（2000）中，"能力"被定义为获得知识、应用知识、分析问题、独立提出观点和创新性。简言之，就是在跨文化语境下通过语言完成任务的能力，这也与本书中ICC的概念不谋而合。换句话说，21世纪的外语人才应具备跨文化沟通能力（ICC）。

大学是一个使学生为职业生涯做准备的机构。因此，使学生具备满足社会需求的素质是大学所应有之责任。从这个意义上说，外语教学作为培养专业外语人才的领域，也应该进行改革以适应社会发展的要求。

随着经济和社会的发展，我国的大学英语教学取得了丰硕的成果。我们的大学英语教师数量不断增加（徐，2006）。专家学者们编写的各类英语教材纷纷由各大出版社出版，例如上海外语教育出版社、高等教育出版社、外语教学与研究出版社等。大学英语课程的教学质量也有了大幅度提升。在20世纪80年代，大多数大学生几乎很难开口说和理解英语。现在他们中的大多数人都能用英语正常交流。总而言之，我国大学英语教学取得了长足的进步。然而，传统外语教学过分强调语言能力。语言是一种沟通的工具，它无法解决跨文化交际中因文化差异而产生的所有问题。因此，经过十多年的英语学习，学生英语读写能力强，但交流能力很弱。换言之，仅有语言教学或训练不足以帮助学生有效地完成跨文化交际活动。从这个意义上说，我们进行本研究旨在寻求一种全新的外语教学理念，它能够通过语言教学这个手段来提高外语学习者的跨文化沟通能力。

我国的外语教学已应用过许多理论和方法，如语法翻译法、直接法和听说法，它们为我国的外语教学做出了巨大的贡献。众所周知，外语教学旨在满足社会对外语人才的需求。因此，外语教学方法的改革也应该跟上社会发展的脚步。21世纪以全球化和多元文化为特征，这就意味着各个领域的人才都应该具备在跨文化背景下工作的能力和素养。跨文化沟通能力是21世纪外语人才的必备条件。因此，跨文化外语教学法的目标是培养外语学习者的跨文化沟通能力。此外，在阐述跨文化外语教学法关键构成要素的基础上，作者进行了实证研究，以检验其有效性。具体而言，本研究将完成以下任务：

（1）提出跨文化外语教学法的概念。

（2）构建跨文化外语教学法体系，包括理论背景、理论方法、教学目标、教材、教学方法、课堂技巧等。

（3）进行跨文化外语教学法的实证研究，以证明其有效性。

本书共分5章。第1章是本书的总览，介绍了研究背景、研究目的和研究意义。第2章介绍了本研究的主要观点，回顾了国际知名学者对跨文化沟通能力及其构成要素，以及外语教学方法的研究现状，分析了跨文化沟通能力与外语教学（FLT）的关系，提出了跨文化沟通能力的概念和构成要素。第3章是本书的核心部分，提出了跨文化外语教学法的概念。基于它的理论背景，作者构建了跨文化外语教学法的体系，阐述了它的教学目标、途径和课堂实施方法。第4章主要介绍了跨文化外语教学法的实证研究。第5章以信息技术的发展为背景，探讨了跨文化外语教学法未来将要面临的挑战和创新发展问题。

很多人为本书的成功出版做出了重要的贡献。非常感谢上海大学庄恩平教授，他是我的研究生导师，也是我进入跨文化交际研究领域的领路人。在他的指导和帮助下，我发现了自己的兴趣，并逐步将学习和研究的重点放在了外语教学中的跨文化交际问题上，这也是我目前一直从事的研究方向。

还要感谢胡燕老师，她是我的同事、朋友和难得的合作伙伴。她几乎参加了我所有项目的研究。她的勤奋、合作和诚恳的态度使我们在外语教学研究中取得了一个又一个成功，她也为本书的出版提出了许多宝贵的建议。

最后，要感谢我的家人，特别是当我在美国密西西比学院做访问学者时，我的父母和儿子对我的陪伴。那段难忘的时期，也是对该书的创作与出版至关重要的时期。

希望本书能对外语教学领域的跨文化沟通研究做出贡献。

吕宁

2023 年 3 月

Preface

In 1964, Canadian communication scholar Marshall McLuhan coined the famous term "global village" to foresee that the world would develop into a small village (McLuhan, 1964). According to him, it is people's communication way, not the highly – developed media that makes the world smaller. Today, McLuhan's prediction is coming true. The communication between different countries and different cultures is popularized on a large scale. Intercultural activities like intercultural cooperation, intercultural aid, intercultural exchange, multinational corporations, international business, intercultural marriage, interpersonal communication, have been an indispensable part of our life. Everything is becoming more and more international and intercultural. Just like Chen (2005) said: "globalization has broken through the boundaries of space, time, cultural assumptions and the scope, structure, and function of human society." This challenge makes intercultural communication competence (ICC) a crucial factor for talents in the job market. Especially, foreign language talents who are fluent in one or more languages can hardly survive in the international competitive environment. Today if studying job advertisements, we can easily find that ICC is a much-demanded qualification in the job market. Kobrin (1984) surveyed 217 American international companies and found that intercultural competence ("international expertise" in his words) was important to many companies when employing people for international jobs and in promotion issues (ibid). Similarly, a survey was done by Chinese Higher Education Committee of Foreign Language Major among employment units covering the areas of ministries, committees, state – owned enterprises, foreign trade companies, and educational departments. The result revealed that the employers' demand for graduates of foreign language major has decreased to zero. 66% of the employers surveyed hoped that foreign – language – major students widen their knowledge scope. Therefore foreign–language–major students are losing their advantage over other majors in the job market.

Meanwhile, *Teaching Syllabus for English Majors in Higher Education Institutions* (2000) listed five kinds of qualities that should be possessed by foreign language talents in the 21st century (It will be elaborated in detail in Chapter 3): the solid language foundation, wide knowledge scope, some major knowledge, higher competence and better qualification. They sound very general. Whereas, in the *Teaching Syllabus for English Majors in Higher Education Institutions* (2000), the "competence" was defined as the ability to acquire knowledge, apply knowledge, analyze questions, propose ideas independently, and be innovative. Accordingly, they can be concluded as the ability to accomplish tasks through language in the intercultural context, which is in accordance with the concept of ICC in my sense. In other words, the foreign language talents of the 21st century should be equipped with ICC.

University is an institution where students prepare for their vocation. Therefore it is the university's responsibility to make the students qualified enough to meet the social demand. In this sense, foreign language teaching (FLT), as a field to cultivate foreign language talents, should be reformed to meet the social requirements.

With the development of economy and society, college English teaching in

China has achieved fruitful results. Now we have more than fifty thousand college English teachers (Xu, 2006). Various English textbooks have been written by scholars and published by publishing groups such as Shanghai Foreign Language Education Press, High Education Press, and Foreign Language Teaching and Research Press. The teaching quality has been improved on a large scale. In the 1980s, most college students could hardly speak and understand English. Now the majority of them can communicate with English-speaking people. Generally speaking, college English teaching in China has made great progress. However, the traditional FLT overemphasizes the language competence. Language acts as a tool for communication, but can never solve all the problems caused by cultural differences arising from intercultural communication. As a result, after more than ten years' study of English, students are efficient in reading and writing in English but deficient in communicating with foreigners. In other words, language teaching or training is not enough to help the students finish intercultural communication activities effectively. In this sense, we conduct the present study to seek FLT concept which can improve language learners' ICC by means of language teaching.

Many theories and methods have been applied to China's FLT, for example, grammar-translation method, direct method, and audiolingual method. They have made great contributions in China's foreign language teaching. It is known that FLT aims to satisfy the social demand for foreign language talents. Hence the reform of FLT methodology should keep pace with the development of society. The 21st century is characterized by globalization and multiculturalism, which means talents in every field should be competent enough to work in an intercultural context. In other words, ICC is the demanding qualification for the foreign language talents of the 21st century. Therefore the goal of intercultural approach to FLT is to cultivate foreign language learners' ICC—a comprehensive system of competence. Furthermore based on expounding the key elements of intercultural approach to FLT, the author has conducted an empirical study to test its effectiveness. In specific, the present study aims to fulfill the following tasks:

(1) To propose the concept of intercultural approach to FLT.

(2) To construct the system of intercultural approach to ELT including its theoretical background, methods, teaching objectives, course books, teaching methods, classroom techniques, etc.

(3) To conduct an experimental application of intercultural approach to FLT to approve its effectiveness.

The book is composed of five chapters. Chapter 1 presents a bird's-eye view of the study, covering the background, objectives and the significance of the study. Chapter 2 presents the view of this study, in which the definitions and components of ICC and some famous FLT pedagogies are reviewed. The relationship between ICC and FLT is analyzed. Chapter 3 is the key part of this book which proposes the new concept of intercultural approach to FLT. Based on the theoretical backgrounds, the author constructs the system of intercultural approach to FLT and elaborates its objectives, channels and classroom methods. Besides, a pedagogical experiment of intercultural approach to FLT is included in this Chapter. Chapter 4 is devoted to an experimental study of intercultural approach to FLT in the classroom to prove it's effectiveness. In Chapter 5, intercultural approach to FLT is discussed on the background of information technology in digital time. It will welcome more challenges and new development.

This book would not have been possible without the contributions of a great many people. I am most grateful to Professor Zhuang Enping, who was my supervisor at Shanghai University. He introduced me to the systematic research of intercultural communication. With his instruction and help, I found my interest and step by step focused my study on IC in foreign language teaching, which is what I am doing now.

I would like to thank Miss Huyan, who is my colleague, friend, and precious partner. She joined almost all the projects and researches I have ever done. She is so hard-working, cooperative, and kind that we achieved our goals successfully in the study of foreign language teaching. She made many excellent suggestions.

Last but not least, I appreciate my family's love for me. Especially when I worked as a visiting scholar at Mississippi College, my parents and my son accompanied me in the United States of America for 2 years. That was an unforgettable period, which was very important to the writing of the book.

I hope that this book does make a contribution to the field of intercultural communication study for foreign language teachers.

Lü Ning

Match, 2023

Contents

Chapter 1 The History of Foreign Language Teaching (FLT)

FLT is a systematic effort by a teacher to induce the learning of a foreign language by one or more students who are native speakers of a different language or languages (Xu, 2006). Chinese FLT has a history of over 700 years (Chen, Fan, Zhong, 2006). There is evidence that the earliest foreign language school in China was established in the Yuan Dynasty in 1289 (ibid). However, it was not until 1903 that English as a foreign language teaching (EFLT) became popular (ibid). After the founding of the People's Republic of China in 1949, college English teaching has undergone over 50 years. A lot of teaching theories and methods have been adopted in FLT. Nowadays, with English becoming an important tool for international communication, EFLT is facing a serious challenge in the globalized world. It is an urgent task to make EFLT serve social development more effectively and sufficiently. Therefore the research of EFLT has attracted more and more scholars' attention. Thus, in this book, FLT mainly refers to EFLT. Before discussing the various EFLT methods, it is necessary to understand and distinguish several key terms.

1.1 The approach, method, and technique

In describing the method, the difference between a philosophy of language teaching at the level of theory and principles, and a set of derived procedures for teaching a language, is central (Richards & Rodgers, 2000). In other words, at different levels of language teaching, the teaching method denotes itself in different forms. American applied linguist Edward Anthony (1963) proposed a scheme to clarify the difference among approach, method and technique. According to Anthony, the approach, method, and technique have different connotations and represent three levels of conceptualization and organization of language teaching.

"... An approach is a set of correlative assumptions dealing with the nature of language teaching and learning. . . "

"... A method is an overall plan for the orderly presentation of language material, no part of which contradicts, and all of which is based upon, the selected approach. . . "

"... A technique is implementational—which actually takes place in a classroom. It is a particular trick, stratagem, or contrivance used to accomplish an immediate objective. . . " (Anthony, 1963)

In terms of degrees of abstraction and specificity, an approach has the highest degree of abstraction at which the nature and assumption of subject matter are described. Alternatively, an approach refers to the theory of language teaching and learning. A method is a middle term which puts the theory into practice. If the approach is an axiom, the method is a procedure to realize the axiom (ibid). A technique is the most specific one which implements methods in classroom. Anthony's scheme serves as a helpful instrument to understand the subject of the present study.

1. 2　FLT methods mainly used in China

Many different theories and methods have ever appeared in the history of foreign language teaching. They emerged to meet the social demand of a certain period and were replaced with the development of our society. In order to achieve a better understanding of intercultural approach to FLT, it is necessary to review the foreign language teaching methods that have a great influence on the development of China's FLT.

1. 2. 1　The grammar-translation method

Although English is the most widely used language in the world today, Latin is the dominating language in western society five hundred years ago (Richards & Rodgers, 2000). People use Latin in almost every aspect of their life, for example, education, commerce, government, religion. Consequently translating written materials from their mother language, such as German, French, Italian, into Latin was an urgent demand in people's life. The model of foreign language study was learning classical Latin and analyzing its grammar. Although in the 16th Latin's dominance in Europe has gradually diminished, the method based on the study of Latin is reserved and become the standard way of studying foreign language in schools.

In the grammar-translation method, the first language is maintained as the reference of massive translation practice (Stern, 2000). The principle feature of grammar-translation method is indicated in its name. It emphasizes teaching the grammar of the foreign language with little attention to speaking and listening to it. Its principle technique is the translation from the native language into the target language. The students are expected to study and memorize the rules of grammar. The exercises appear mainly in two forms: translation into the target language and translation into the first language.

Grammar – translation method dominated European and foreign language teaching from the 1840s to the 1940s, and in modified form it continues to be widely used in some parts of the world today. In the mid and late 19th century, opposition to the grammar-translation method gradually developed in several European countries (ibid). It gradually vanished from the controlling position of FLT.

In China, the grammar-translation method made a great contribution to the training of translators. Before the reform and opening up, there were a lot of materials in foreign languages that needed to be translated into Chinese. However, not many scientific personnel could understand them, which led to the urgent need for translators. Thus the objective of foreign language teaching was to train a large number of translators. That is why the grammar – translation method was prevalent in FLT of that period.

1. 2. 2 The direct method

After the 1850s, a language teaching reform happened particularly in Europe (Richards & Rodgers, 2000). Many specialists like Marcel, Gouin, Sweet attempted to change the traditional grammar – translation method to make language teaching more efficient (ibid). What they proposed is called the "natural" method. Gouin had been one of the first of the nineteenth-century reformers to attempt to build a methodology around observation of child language learning (ibid). Sauveur (1826—1907) used intensive oral interaction in target language teaching and employed questions as a way of presenting and eliciting language (ibid). Some other believers in the "natural" methods argued that a foreign language could be taught without translation or the use of the learner's native tongue if meaning was conveyed directly through demonstration and action (ibid). The direct method was built on the foundation of these natural language learning principles.

"Direct" means direct learning, direct understanding and direct application (Stern, 2000). The direct method emphasizes the teaching of oral language and phonetics. The target language is used as a means of instruction and communication in the language classroom, and the use and translation of the native language is avoided. The standard classroom activity is the presentation of the text by the teacher. In order to explain the meaning of the text, the teachers ask questions about it, and the students read aloud for practice. The students are encouraged to find the grammatical rules involved in the text by themselves. Besides, As Stern (2000) said, "The direct method represents a shift from literary language to the spoken everyday language as the object of early instruction, a goal that is totally lacking in grammar-translation."

1. 2. 3 The audio-lingual method

Under the influence of structuralism and psychology, the audio‑lingual method interprets the process of language learning in terms of stimulus and response (Stern, 2000). Thus the audio-lingual method throws emphasis on the fundamental language skills, i. e. , listening and speaking that precede reading and writing in the teaching sequence. In operation, the students are required to repeatedly practice pattern drills. And the dialogues displayed by tape recorders and language laboratory are the main contents of teaching. Like the direct method, it highlights oral training and advocates the development of target language skills without reference to the native tongue. Besides, it has several features:

(1) Although language is infinite and complicated, it can be concluded as finite pattern drills. Through inferring from the patterns, the students will be able to understand and express infinite sentences. Therefore pattern drills are the center of the audio-lingual method.

(2) Language is a kind of habit and the form of the habit depends a lot on a large quantity of practice.

(3) In the teaching procedure of the audio-lingual method, the class is filled with active and simple practice. The memorization of dialogues and imitative repetition are its featured teaching techniques (ibid).

1. 2. 4 The audiovisual method or the situational method

In the 1970s, the audio-lingual method characterized by mechanical drill practice can not satisfy people's requirement for foreign language (Stern, 2000). A new method succeeding the audio-lingual method and the direct method was developed in France. It is called audiovisual method or situational method which highlights language's structure on the theoretical basis of structuralism. The name of audiovisual method contains dualistic meanings. One is the application of audio and visual equipments and techniques. The other is that students' listening comprehension can only be achieved by exposure to the holistic structure of the language. The holistic structure refers to the integration of a situation or a picture and a group of words and meanings.

Similar to the audio-lingual method, the audiovisual method or situational method also makes speaking ability the primary target of teaching. While it emphasizes training students' language skills: listening, speaking, reading and writing, in a real or social situation. That is, language is combined with the situation of language use so that language teaching approaches to the conversation in natural situation. Accordingly, the teaching content mainly consists of various dialogues happening in our daily life. The teacher employs the visually presented scenario by modern equipments to improve students' language skills in daily situations. This method has a great influence on Chinese English teaching. Many English course books were compiled according to the principles of the audiovisual method, such as *New Concept English*.

Since the end of the 1970s, China has carried out the policy of reform and opening up. The strategies of "going out" and "coming in" have motivated the exchange of science and technology at home and abroad. China's learning from the west has not been restricted to the translation of their documentation. Many talents have been sent to study abroad. Meanwhile, more and more enterprises began to expand their market outside China. Under this circumstance, the foreign language talents were required to communicate directly with foreigners in the exchange and negotiations. Their primary qualification of translation was replaced by the speaking and listening ability. The adoption of the above methods in China's FLT helped to enhance the qualification of foreign language talents, especially their speaking and listening abilities.

1. 2. 5 The communicative approach

The communicative approach in language teaching started from a theory of language as communication (Richards & Rodgers, 2000). In 1965, Chomsky used competence and performance to signify an ideal speakers' language learning. By competence, he referred to the perfect knowledge of an ideal speaker — listener of the language in a homogeneous speech community. In other words, the linguistic competence including the native speakers' knowledge of his own language and the system of internalized rules about the language enables the speaker to create new grammatical sentences and reject the ambiguous and ungrammatical ones. Hymes opposed Chomsky's competence and performance model. He proposed the term "communicative competence", which was "the ability not only to apply the grammatical rules of a language in order to form grammatically correct sentences but also to know when and where to use these sentences and to whom" (Xu, 2006). According to Hymes (1972), if a person possessed communicativd competence, he would acquire both knowledge and ability for language use. Canale and Swain (1980) specified communicative competence as grammatical competence, discourse competence, sociolinguistic competence and strategic competence. The first two components represent the use of the linguistic system. The last two components deal with the functional aspects of communication. The ultimate goal of communicative language teaching is to develop students' communicative competence. Just as Jeremy Harmer (1991) said, "The communicative approach is anumbrella term to describe methodology by which teachers teach studentshow to communicate efficiently and which also lays emphasis on theteaching of communicative value and, in some cases, the teaching of language functions. " Therefore, the classroom of communicative teaching is more like the world outside the classroom where people use language spontaneously and communicatively (Xu, 2006). The students are offered ample opportunities to use the language for communicative purposes. Many activities, such as role – play, group talk, are arranged by the teacher to encourage cooperative and communicative practice.

The period during the 1990s sees the booming of China's development. With the excellent performance of reform and opening up, China's economy entered the period with unprecedented prosperity. Many countries and regions have established business relationships with China, which is becoming one of the most potential markets in the world. Owing to the profitable policy and rich source of talent, a number of foreign companies have come to invest and some international corporations built their branches in our country. Economic development has fostered educational reform, especially in English education. The communicative approach has been employed widely in FLT to train foreign language learners' communicative competence, i. e. language competence.

This is a brief review of the FLT methods mainly used in our country. Every method or approach has its specific objectivs and serves the certain demand of social development. Undoubtedly they were also reformed, even replaced by the change of the social situation. In the 21st century, the trend of globalization exposes foreign language talents to a multi-cultural atmosphere. Language competence is not enough to enable foreign language talents to survive the challenge. The 21st century demands foreign language talents who can fulfill tasks in the intercultural context, namely talents with intercultural communication competence (ICC). Therefore the reform of FLT pedagogy is imperative under the situation. *Higher Education Committee of Foreign Language Major about the reform of foreign language teaching of the 21st century certain opinions* (1998), pointed out that the cultivating mode of foreign language talents has not adapted to the changing social situation. In fact, the new surge of FLT reform has come into being in the western countries. Byram (1995) has manifested: "The greatest shift towards the new concept in foreign language pedagogy with a view to incorporating the new conditions in Europe today is the replacement of communicative competence as an objective with the desire to achieve a much broader intercultural competence. " American FLT objectives in the 21st century are concluded as five C's: communication, cultures, connections, comparisons, communities (Chen, Fan, Zhong, 2006).

Chapter 2　Intercultural Communication Competence（ICC）

Weste rnresearchers became interested in ICC in the late 1950s and early 1960s（Arasaratnam, 2003）. During the 1980s and 1990s, ICC has been studied extensively bysociologists, psychologists, sociolinguists, interculturalists, etc. , in various contexts such as sojourner adaptation, acculturation, international culture and business communication, cross－cultural counseling etc. （ibid）. While in China, it was not until the late 1970s and early 1980s that the study of intercultural communication was started by introducing western theories and research achievements. In this section, the review of ICC research will be divided into two parts: western scholars' study and Chinese scholars' study. Each part will be followed by the author's discussion as the conclusion. Besides, the researches of scholars from both areas will be compared and their differences will be analyzed for the present study.

2. 1 Western researchers' study on ICC

2. 1. 1 The definitions of ICC

Although "the study of communication competence could be indirectly traced back to Aristotle's rhetoric"（Chen, 1990）, the concept of communica-

10

tive competence was firstly proposed by Hymes on the basis of criticizing Chomsky's theory. In 1965, Chomsky established the theory of competence and performance. According to him, competence refers to a speaker's knowledge of the rules of his native language, while performance is the actual application of these rules. Chomsky takes an ideal native speaker as the subject of competence who only constructs and recognizes grammatical sentences. Therefore this kind of competence can hardly be achieved.

Chomsky's notion of competence was challenged by many scholars. They thought that Chomsky neglected the social and cultural significance of an utterance in the situation and context in which it was used. In 1972, Hymes published his book *On Communicative Competence*, in which he defined communicative competence as a speaker's grammatical, psychological, social and cultural knowledge and his ability to use the knowledge. In his opinion, language is not an independent system. Instead, it should be inseparable from culture. Thus it is evident that the status of culture in language teaching was theoretically questioned when the notion of communicative competence was put forward.

Hymes' theory provides us a wider view to understand competence. However he did not describe the application of "communicative competence" in practice. In other words, people can hardly achieve the communicative competence as Hymes' description. In 1980, Canaleand Swain put forward a more practical model which included grammatical competence, sociolinguistic competence, discourse competence and strategic competence. The model is based on Hymes' communicative competence, but makes it more operable and realizable.

According to Canale and Swain (1980), grammatical competence refers to the language code which includes "vocabulary and rules of word formation, pronunciation, spelling, sentence formation and linguistic semantics" (Canale,

1983). It was called "linguistic competence" by Chomsky. Sociolinguistic competence refers to "the extent to which utterances are produced and understood appropriately in different sociolinguistic contextual factors such as status of participants, purpose of the interaction, and norms or conventions of interaction" (ibid). Discourse competence refers to "mastery of how to combine grammatical forms and meanings to achieve a unified spoken or written text in different genres" (ibid). Strategic competence consists of verbal and nonverbal communication strategies that may be used to compensate for breakdowns and misunderstanding in communication.

From the early study of ICC, we can find that most researchers are linguists so language ability is the focus of their research. However Byram (1991) had pointed out that "experience and studies have ascertained that the educational system and foreign language courses do not prevent problems arising from misunderstandings which are best characterized as 'cultural' rather than just linguistic misinterpretations". It therefore is necessary to find out new objectives for acquiring a competence which may enhance the possibilities of mutual understanding in intercultural situations and facilitate the language learner's meeting with other cultures. In addition, the concept of communicative competence is based on "a native-speaker ideal, i. e. a native-speaker in interaction with another native-speaker" (Byram, 1995). The objective of competence training should reflect the reality of a foreign language speaker using the foreign language for communication and interaction with members of another culture. Thus with the development of intercultural study, not only linguists but also sociologists, psychologists etc. began to participate in the academic research of intercultural communication. As a result, the concept of ICC was developed to a broader sense.

Ruben's studies are two of the earliest investigations on the concept of ICC

(Chen, G. M. 1992). He defined communication competence, based on which he identified seven behavioral elements of ICC that make an individual function effectively in intercultural settings. He also designed an instrument of measuring ICC named Intercultural Behavioral Assessment Indices (IBAI). According to Ruben (1976), communication competence is "the ability to function in a manner that is perceived to be relatively consistent with the needs, capacities, goals, and expectations of the individuals in one's environment while satisfying one's own needs, capacities, goals, and expectation". It is mainly from a behavioral perspective. In this definition, individual behaviors and skills in the process of intercultural interaction are emphasized. The behavioral effectiveness is the core criterion of intercultural communication.

Spitzberg (1988) defined ICC from a social perspective. He regarded "competent communication" as "interaction that is perceived as effective in fulfilling certain rewarding objectives in a way that is also appropriate to the context in which the interaction occurs." By the key word "perceived", Spitzberg suggested that "communicative competence is a social judgment about how well a person interacts with others" (Lustig, 1999). In other words, intercultural competence (IC) involves "a social perception that is always specific to the context and interpersonal relationship within which it occurs" (ibid). Because competence involves interaction between people, competent interpersonal communication results in appropriate and effective behaviors.

Similarly "effective" and "appropriate" are stressed in Chen and Starosta's definition of ICC (1998). They think that ICC is "the ability to effectively and appropriately execute communication behaviors to elicit a desired response in a specific environment". In other words, competent persons must not only know how to interact effectively and appropriately with people and environment, but also know how to fulfill their own communication goals using this ability.

Kim (1991) offered a more detailed definition: ICC is "the overall internal capability of an individual to manage key challenging features of intercultural communication: namely, cultural differences and unfamiliarity, inter-group posture, and the accompanying experience of stress". Accordingly, ICC is people's intrinsic ability which enables them to deal with various intercultural situations. The core of the ability lies in the adaptability. That is, facing specific intercultural communicative activities, competent communicators should adjust themselves flexibly and appropriately. Thus Kim defined ICC mainly from a socio-psychological perspective.

From the viewpoint of Paige (2003), IC means having the knowledge, commitment, compassion, and practical skills to effectively function in and respond to: culturally diverse environments and their challenges; culturally diverse persons/groups and their needs; cultural constructions that privilege some but not others—this means recognizing, deconstructing, and contesting privilege.

We are more inclined to Meyer's definition (1991) of IC.

Intercultural competence, as part of a broader foreign speaker competence, identifies the ability of a person to behave adequately and in a flexible manner when confronted with actions, attitudes and expectations of representatives of foreign cultures.

Meanwhile, he elaborated adequacy and flexibility as the awareness of the cultural differences between one's own and the foreign culture and the ability to handle cross-cultural problems which result from these differences (ibid). The latter ability corresponds with what we claim for ICC.

2. 1. 2　The components of ICC

In the effort of conceptualizing ICC, scholars constructed many models to elaborate its components and dimensions for intercultural interactions. Fantini （1994） identified five dimensions: awareness, attitudes, skills, knowledge, and proficiency in the host tongue. Byram （2000） believed that ICC involved five elements: attitude, knowledge, skills of interpreting and relating, skills of discovering and interaction, critical cultural awareness/political education. The following section will be devoted to the ICC models of Spitzberg & Cupaih and Chen which contribute most to the thesis.

2. 1. 2. 1　Spitzberg and Cupaih's model

Spitzberg and Cupach （1984） put up their model of ICC which isolated three components of communication competence: motivation, knowledge, and skills. Motivation refers to our desire to communicate appropriately and effectively with others. According to Lustig and Koester （1999）, motivation includes the overall set of emotional associations that people have as they anticipate and actually communicate interculturally. Knowledge refers to the cognitive information you need to have about the people, the context, and the norms of appropriateness that operate in a specific culture （ibid）. It is our awareness or understanding of what needs to be done in order to communicate appropriately and effectively. IC depends on both cultural−general and cultural−specific information. Skills are our abilities to engage in the behaviors necessary to communicate appropriately and effectively. The three elements are integrated to form the construct of ICC, each of which alone is insufficient to obtain ICC. In other words, a competent intercultural communicator must be highly motivated, has sufficient knowledge and possesses the communication skills. This trichotomy of ICC is one of the most widely used models of ICC.

This trio-model of ICC was approved by many IC scholars. Samovar & Porter (2004) adopted the three elements as the basic components of communication competence. Gudykunst (1992) pointed out that ICC competence should encompass such categories as cognitive, affective and behavioral aspects. Kim specifies three dimensions of ICC: cognitive, emotional and operational. Lustig and Koester (1999) also held that intercultural competence is represented by three dimensions: sufficient knowledge, suitable motivation and skilled action. It can be concluded that affective, cognitive as well as behavioral components must be developed in order to communicate efficiently and properly with individuals from different cultures.

2.1.2.2 Chen Guoming's model

Chen's model of ICC underwent several stages. In 1989, Chen proposed four dimensions of ICC: personal attributes, communication skills, psychological adaptation, and cultural awareness. It is illustrated in Figure 2.1:

(1) Personal attributes—is the affective aspect of ICC, which refers to "the traits that constitute an individual's personality" (Chen, 1989). The main personal traits that affect ICC include self-concept, self-disclosure, self-awareness, and social relaxation.

(2) Communication skills—is the behavioral aspect of ICC, which are "the verbal and nonverbal behaviors that enable us to be effective in interactions with others" (ibid). Message skills, behavioral flexibility, interaction management, and social skills are useful behaviors in ICC.

(3) Psychological adaptation—is the psychological aspect of ICC, referring to "our ability to a new culture" (ibid). This is a crucial part of

```
                                               ┌─ Self-concept
                          Personal Attributes ─┤  Self-disclosure
                                               │  Self-awareness
                                               └─ Social Relaxation
                                               ┌─ Message Skills
                          Communication Skills ┤  Behavioral Flexibility
                                               │  Interaction Management
   Intercultural                               └─ Social Skills
   Communication ─┤                            ┌─ Stress
   Competence                                  │  Frustration
                  Psychological Adaptation ────┤  Alienation
                                               └─ Ambiguity
                                               ┌─ Social Values
                          Cultural Awareness ──┤  Social Customs
                                               │  Social Norms
                                               └─ Social Systems
```

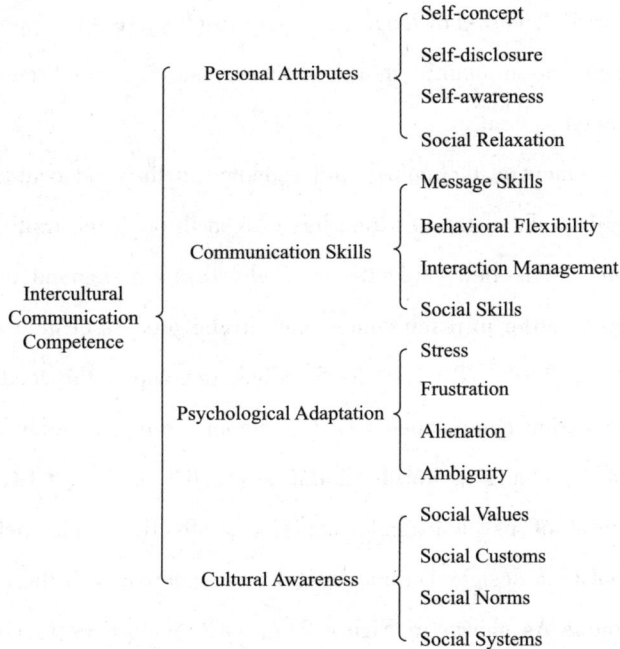

Figure 2. 1　Dimensions and components of ICC（Chen, 1989）

ICC. Lysgaard（1955）had ever proposed the U-curve hypothesis to explain the three steps of psychological adaptation: initial adjustment, crisis, and regained adjustment. He indicated that adjustment does not increase at a constant level（ibid）. Furnham and Bochner（1982）also suggested that the greater difference between the host culture and the home culture, the more difficulties the communicator will face. In general, a competent communicator will possess the ability to deal with stress, feelings of frustration, feelings of alienation, and ambiguous situations caused by the new environment（ibid）.

（4）Cultural awareness—is the cognitive aspect of ICC, which refers to "understanding the conventions of the host culture that affect how people think and behave" (ibid). It corresponds with the knowledge part of Spitzberg and Cupaih's ICC model. The knowledge necessary to effective and appropriate intercultural communication mainly includes social values, social customs, social norms, and social systems.

The development of technology and economy in the 21st century has accelerated the trend of globalization which has broken through the traditional ways of communication. "The new imperatives of globalization demand a new way of communication in order to reach competence in the process of intercultural interaction." (Chen, 2005) Thus in 2005, Chen developed the model of ICC to global communication competence (GCC) model aiming at adjusting people to the demand of the changing world. Similar to the ICC model, GCC is a holistic system consisting of psychological, cognitive, affective, and behavioral levels. However GCC is designed from a broader perspective with the global context as its background. As shown in Figure 2.2, GCC comprises four components: global mindset, unfolding the self, mapping the culture, and aligning the interaction.

As the foundation of GCC, the global mindset refers to openness to other cultures that facilitates intercultural interactions. According to Gupta and Govindarajan (1997), global mindset calls for people to broaden and expand their thinking by eliminating those filters on possesses about other cultures and their differences (ibid). Therefore, as a psychological process, it helps people decrease or avoid ethnocentrism and parochialism in the IC. Unfolding the self represents "individual's personal characteristics, including flexibility, sensitivity, open-mindedness, and motivation. It helps to bridge the gap between the self and the society" (ibid). Besides, GCC requires "the cognitive ability to map one's own and other's cultures and the behavioral skills to accustom individuals to

Global Mindset
- Impel to broaden perspective
- Motivate to respect diversity
- Expect to reconcile conflict
- Propel to regulate change
- Orient to globalizing process

Mapping the Culture
- Bewilderment of the differences
- Frustration of the differences
- Cognitive analysis
- Empathic immersion

Global Communication Competence

Unfolding the Self
- Ceaseless purifying
- Continuous learning
- Cultivate sensitivity
- Develop creativity
- Foster empathy

Aligning the Interaction
- Language ability
- Behavioral flexibility
- Interaction management
- Identity maintenance
- Managing changes

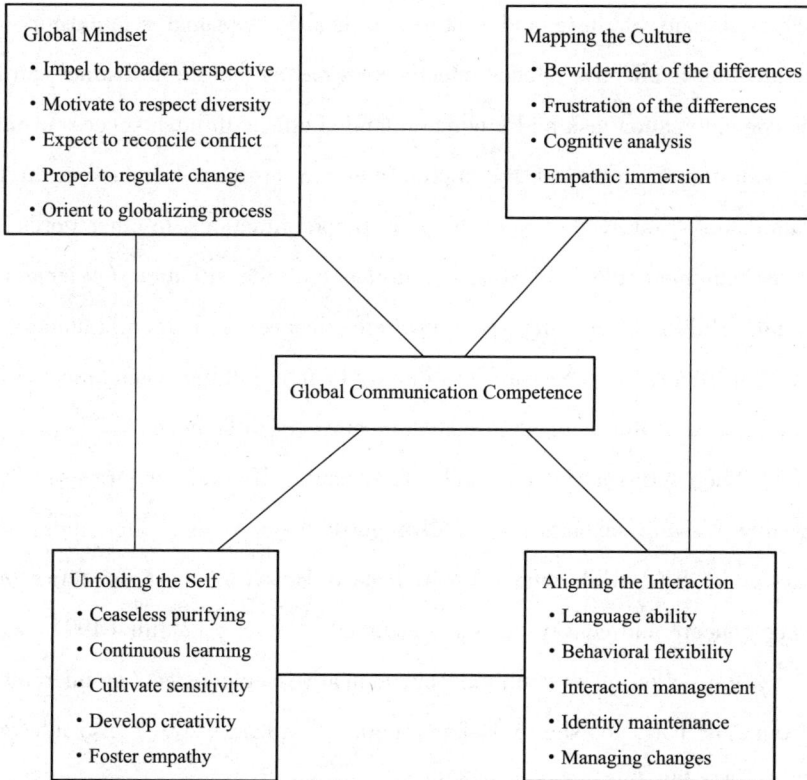

Figure 2. 2 The Model of Global Communication Competence (Chen, 2005)

the globalizing communicative situations" (ibid). GCC broadens the scope of ICC research and provides reference to many Chinese scholars' research on ICC.

2. 1. 3 Discussion on western researches

With an overview of the western scholars' studies on ICC, the following distinctive features are discovered and analyzed as follows:

(1) Two concepts are emphasized—effectiveness and appropriateness. Ac-

cording to Dodd (2006), if a person fulfilled his communication task, adapted himself to the new culture and established healthy personal relationship, his communication is effective. Hence effectiveness means that an individual can fulfill his communication task and produce intended effects through successful interaction with the environment. By appropriateness, western scholars mean that communicators speak or do proper things in proper situations. In other words, interactants can meet the contextual requirement of the situation (Wiemann & Backlund, 1980). Generally speaking, effectiveness and appropriateness are not only the standards to measure the quality of intercultural communication but also the ideal goal that competent communicators try to achieve.

(2) Such terms as intercultural effectiveness, ICC and IC are used interchangeably. Western scholars do not distinguish them. In their literatures, some scholars prefer ICC, while others use IC instead. However, these two terms mean the same concept and convey the same connotation. Even, Fantini (1994) stated that "... the notion of intercultural communicative competence (or intercultural competence or ICC, for short) is fairly new... " . Kim (2001) also advocated that "considerable divergence is seen in the existing academic conceptions of communication competence and intercultural communication competence (or intercultural competence and such related terms as intercultural skills and intercultural effectiveness) " . Moreover, in defining intercultural competence, Samovar (2004) used the definition of intercultural communication competence offered by Spitzberg & Kim for reference. The author is in favor of their treatment to the terms. In this book, ICC is adopted.

(3) The integration of various dimensions is highlighted in constructing ICC. ICC is a comprehensive system involving cognitive level, behavioral level, psychological level, affective level, etc. Competent intercultural communicators

should possess comprehensive abilities. Also it is helpful to broaden the research of ICC. At present, scholars from psychology, sociology, behaviorism, linguistics, etc. are working in the area of intercultural communication with their own academic perspectives and have integrated their research with the study of ICC. Thus, many culture related disciplines have been developed. To some extent, this feature of studies has contributed to the multi-directional trend of ICC research in the western countries.

2.2　Chinese researchers' study on ICC

In the early 1980s, Chinese professor Xu Guozhang proposed that words with equivalent literal meanings may differ in their cultural connotations (Zhuang, 2006). At the end of 1980s, professor Hu Wenzhong introduced some western scholars' ideas and views on intercultural communication study to China, which preluded the beginning of intercultural communication studies in China. After more than 20 years' studies in China, intercultural communication has been established as an independent academic area. The importance of ICC has been gaining increasing attention and many scholars have done lots of research to promote ICC in China. Among them, more influential scholars are Hu Wenzhong, Jia Yuxin, Wen Qiufang, Zhao Aiguo & Jiang Yaming and Yang Ying & Zhuang Enping.

2.2.1　Hu Wenzhong and Gao Yihong's research

Hu Wenzhong and Gao Yihong (1997) put forward the concept of social culture competence (SCC) and constructed its model. From their viewpoint, SCC refers to the ability to apply the acquired knowledge and skill to the process of social cultural information which synthesizes people's personality and develops people's potential. In the model of social culture competence, two core abilities are highlighted: communicative competence and flexibility. The former refers to the basic ability to use language including language ability and pragmatic ability. The latter is the higher qualities of using language including understanding ability, evaluating ability and synthesizing ability (Figure 2.3).

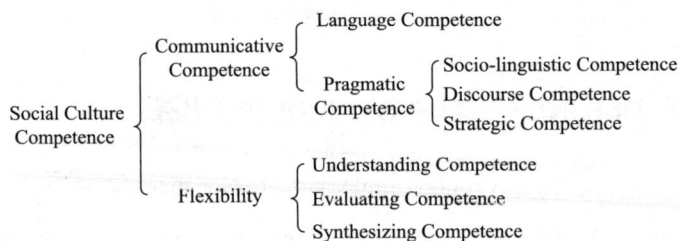

Social Culture Competence
- Communicative Competence
  - Language Competence
  - Pragmatic Competence
    - Socio-linguistic Competence
    - Discourse Competence
    - Strategic Competence
- Flexibility
  - Understanding Competence
  - Evaluating Competence
  - Synthesizing Competence

Figure 2.3 Hu Wenzhong and Gao Yihong's model of SCC (1997)

2.2.2 Jia Yuxin's research

Jia Yuxin (1997) approved Ruben's definition of ICC, but he preferred the name of effective communication competence. In his opinion, communicative competence and effective communication are closely related but different concepts. Communicative competence serves as a prerequisite and guarantee for effective communication. He constructed a more comprehensive model of effective communicative competence (ECC) (Figure 2.4).

Jia Yuxin's model involves four subsystems. The system of basic communication competence refers to language competence necessary to one's effective communication and communicative competence relating to social and cultural norms. In the system of affective and relational competence, affective competence

Effective communication competence
- System of basic communication competence
  - Verbal and nonverbal competence
  - Cultural competence
  - Interactional competence
  - Cognitive competence
- System of affective and relational competence
  - Affectivecompetence : empathy
  - Relational competence
- The episodic competence system
  - Scripts
  - Goals
  - Interaction rules
  - Interaction scene
- The strategic competence system
  - Code switching
  - Approximative strategy
  - Cooperative strategy
  - Nonverbal strategy

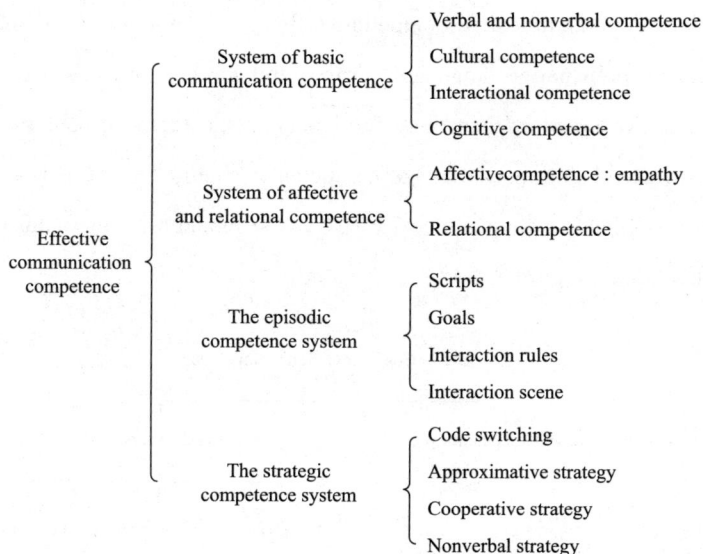

Figure 2. 4   Jia Yuxin's model of ECC（1997）

mainly equals to empathy. The communicators possessing empathy competence can explain and evaluate other people's behavior from their perspective rather than from their own. According to Jia（ibid）, episode means a process of communicators' coordinated actions in a certain context, such as how do communicators coordinate their behavior, how do they know what others are doing, how will they resolve the disagreement between the two parties of communication. The episodic competence system is used to settle the inconsistency happening in communication. The strategic competence system is used to compensate the deficiency of language or pragmatic competence.

2. 2. 3 Wen Qiufang's research

Compared with Jia Yuxin's study, Wen Qiufang（1999）denoted ICC from a more concrete perspective. She thought foreign language competence should not be equivalent to communicative competence. Because communicative competence can be used in both native language learning and foreign language learning. But contrary to native language learning, foreign language learning contains cultural differences. Instead, foreign language competence should be defined as "cross-cultural communication competence" (CCC). A model was also constructed to expound her idea (Figure 2. 5).

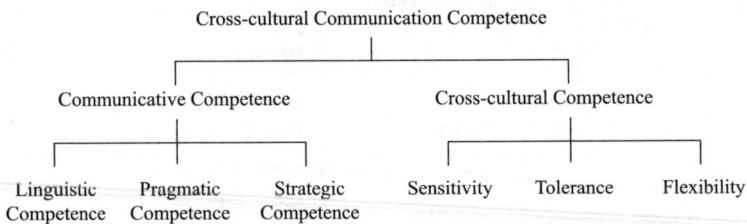

Cross-cultural Communication Competence

Communicative Competence   Cross-cultural Competence

Linguistic   Pragmatic   Strategic   Sensitivity   Tolerance   Flexibility
Competence   Competence   Competence

Figure 2. 5   Wen Qiufang's model of CCC (1999)

In this model, communicative competence mainly refers to the basic language competence and language – using competence. While in the other part, cross – cultural competence refers to the competence of dealing with cultural differences including the sensitivity to cultural differences, tolerance to cultural differences and the flexibility to deal with cultural differences.

2. 2. 4 Zhao Aiguo and Jiang Yaming's research

Zhao Aiguo and Jiang Yaming (2003) thought of ICC as a special concept referring to non – native language or second language communication competence. Thus FLT aims to train students' such qualification that enables them to apply the learned language to intercultural communication. As a result, their model of ICC is specialized in foreign language teaching (Figure 2. 6).

```
                                          ┌ Phonetic Competence
                                          │ Vocabulary Competence
                    ┌ Language Competence ┤
                    │                     │ Grammatical Competence
                    │                     └ Semantic Competence
                    │                     ┌ Contextual Competence
                    │                     │ Discourse Competence
     ICC ┤ Pragmatic Competence ┤
                    │                     │ Sociolinguistic Competence
                    │                     └ Social-cultural Competence
                    │                     ┌ Social Competence
                    └ Behavioral Competence ┤ Nonverbal Competence
                                          └ Cultural Adaptation Competence
```

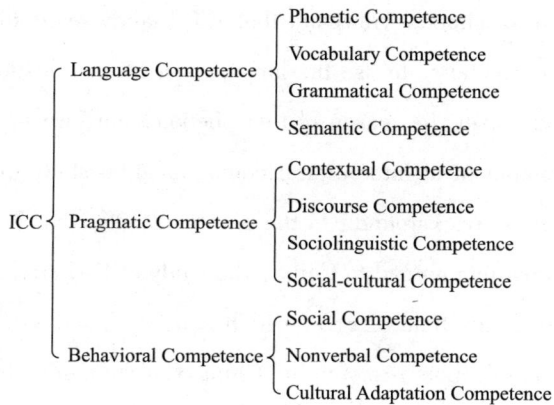

Figure 2. 6　Zhao Aiguo and Jiang Yaming's model of ICC（2003）

2. 2. 5　Yang Ying and Zhuang Enping's ICC model

Yang Ying and Zhuang Enping（2007）constructed the ICC Framework for FLT. According to them, language competence is just the channel or instrument to achieve ICC, and the object of FLT should train students' ICC. Their views are supported in this book and their model will be discussed in detail in Chapter 3.

2. 2. 6　Discussion on Chinese researches

Through the overview of Chinese scholars' researches, several distinctive features are also demonstrated:

（1）Language competence is the core of the ICC researches. Language competence is emphasized in almost all the above studies. Particularly, in Wen Qiufang's model, the three components of communicative competence are all about language and its application. Even Zhao Aiguo and Jiang Yaming equate ICC with foreign language communication competence. Therefore it can be concluded from Chinese scholars' viewpoint that ICC mainly refers to language competence and the competence to use the language in communication.

In order to discover the reason of this phenomenon, we need to look back on the early development of intercultural communication study in China and the researchers' academic background. On the one hand, after Hu Wenzhong's introducing ICC theories from abroad to China, the study of ICC originated and developed prosperously in the field of FLT, which can be named as the birthplace of intercultural communication research in China. Consequently the achievements were mainly used in language teaching practice. On the other hand, most researchers of ICC are foreign language teachers with linguistic background. Hu Wenzhong, Jia Yuxin and Wen Qiufang are all professors of foreign language school of their universities. Zhao Aiguo and Jiang Yaming graduated from Russian linguistics major. Therefore, it is inevitable to reflect their academic background in the ICC research. Comparatively the western scholars have various academic backgrounds, such as psychology, business, communication, sociology, etc. Hu Wenzhong (2005) has ever surveyed the background of the authors who published papers in *International Journal of Intercultural Relations* (IJIR), an authoritative journal of America, from 1999 to 2002. The result is shown in Table 2. 1.

Table 2. 1 Result of Hu Wenzhong's survey

Academic Background	Number of Authors	Percentage of Authors
Psychology	46	30. 46%
Communication	30	19. 87%
Business Management	22	14. 57%
Education	9	5. 96%
Others	34	22. 52%
Unknown	10	6. 62%

To be brief, most researchers are language teachers and their achievements are mainly applied to language teaching in China, which makes a tend-
ency that ICC research will be narrowed down to a language oriented research. Comparing with the western researches, ICC studies in China displays
many limitations.

（2）Various concepts such as cross-cultural communication competence,
effective communication competence are used to signify ICC. However, ICC and
IC are treated differently and seldom used interchangeably. Yangying and Zhuang
Enping（2007）have concluded the four ways used by Chinese scholars for these
two terms.

• Only discussing ICC without mentioning IC. It is one of the most popular
methods of dealing with different terms, such as Zhao and Jiang's research.

• Making IC a branch of ICC. A distinctive example is Wen Qiufang's
Cross-cultural Communication Competence in which cross-cultural competence is
one of the two key elements.

• Treating ICC and IC respectively, but avoiding their relations. Bi Jiwan
（2005）concluded the three cores of ICC research as IC, social cultural competence and ICC.

• IC takes the place of ICC but it is not given any explanation in some
scholars' research. Liu Qisheng（2004）Pointed out, IC is the competence
to use language appropriately and to communicate in foreign language context.

Chinese scholars' research on ICC is still in an exploratory stage. A lot of
work needs our effort in order to keep pace with the world mainstream of ICC research.

2. 3 ICC in FLT

FLT is the field of language training and teaching. The close relationship between language and culture makes culture a necessary part of language teaching. The ability to communicate among different cultures is called ICC. Thus the training of ICC is indivisible from FLT.

In China, the study of intercultural communication mainly attract the interest of foreign language teachers. FLT is the field that predominates in China's intercultural communication research. According to Hu Wenzhong's statistics (2005), 5333 articles have been published in Chinese academic journals from 1979 to 2006, most of which were focused on FLT. The author has also surveyed the papers on ICC published in Chinese academic journals from 2000 to 2006. The result has showed that 80. 65% of the total 2238 papers are studies of ICC within FLT. They have provided a wealth resource for our research. Therefore FLT can serve as an important area of ICC research and its application.

In addition, with the development of globalization, training students' ICC should be recognized as the objective of FLT. *English-teaching Syllabus for English Majorsin Higher Institutions* (2000) stated for the first time that English teachers should attach more importance to the training of ICC. In 2004, *Requests for College English Course* was carried out and it also claimed that intercultural communication should be included in college English teaching.

However, teaching practice in this field is far from satisfactory. (Wu, 2006) Zhuang Enping has conducted an investigation in Shanghai Foreign service Company and Shanghai Foreign Affaires Office for intercultural communication competence of English major graduates. The result showed that in terms of job performance in the intercultural context, English – major graduates did not display great advantage over the graduates of other majors. What leads to the embarrassment of foreign – language – major students? On the one hand, language competence is overemphasized in the current FLT. However, language can not resolve all the problems arising from intercultural communication. On the other hand, to most foreign language teachers, the training of ICC actually refers to the introduction of cultural knowledge, such as political system, habits, customs. In order to do the job well in the intercultural context, students should know how to solve problems with appropriate and effective communication in the multi–cultural context. Therefore in the present study, the author proposes intercultural approach to FLT that aims to improve student' ICC in the course of FLT.

Chapter 3 Intercultural Approach to FLT

The analysis of the job markets and the FLT syllabus make it clear that the 21st century needs foreign language talents to possess ICC. However, the current teaching practice in China is focused on language competence without paying enough attention to training students' ICC. As a result, it is common that students are strong in linguistic competence or even communicative competence, but weak in intercultural communication competence. In order to satisfy the social requirement for intercultural communication competence personnel, a reform in FLT methodology is necessary and urgent. Therefore this book intends to shed light on the notion that education serves society or produces market – needed personnel. Realizing the challenging China FLT is facing, the book calls for the necessary adjustment or change in China FLT for its objective or its methodology. According to Edward Anthony's theory, intercultural approach to FLT, as an approach, aims to develop foreign language learners' ICC by means of language training. As a method, the training of learners' ICC should be reflected in the teaching process of different language skill courses, such as intensive reading, extensive reading, listening, speaking, writing, translation. In classroom teaching, five techniques are put forward to realize the objective of ICC. In this Chapter, such details of intercultural approach to FLT as its background, theoretical foundations, methods, course books, teachers, etc. will be discussed.

3. 1 Concept of foreign language talents

3. 1. 1 An analysis of the syllabus

FLT aims to satisfy the social requirements of foreign language talents. What kind of foreign language talents should FLT cultivate to serve society? In other words, what is the objective of FLT? The FLT syllabus and some documents issued by the Chinese Educational Department have issued different statements in the different periods of social development.

In 1986, *College English Syllabus* (For Students of Arts and Sciences) stated: "College English teaching aims to develop students' relatively high level of competence in reading, an intermediate level of competence in listening and a basic competence in writing and speaking. After the completion of the course, students should be able to use the English language they have learned as a means to obtain whatever information they need in their fields of specialization and also as a solid foundation for further improvement of their command of the language." It is shown that language competence, especially reading ability, was highlighted while ICC was not mentioned in this version.

In *English - teaching Syllabus for English Majors in Higher Institutions* (2000), the objective of EFT was described as cultivating compounded English talents who possess a solid English language foundation and extensive cultural knowledge and who are skilled in using English for the job of translation, teaching, management and research in such fields as foreign affairs, education, business and trade, culture, science and technology, military affairs. Accordingly, the emphasis on English talents' competence was changed from reading ability in

College English Syllabus (For Students of Arts and Sciences) to the ability of using language. In addition, it is worth noting that in this syllabus, cultural knowledge is added to the objective of EFLT and ICC is mentioned for the first time although it is confined to knowledge introduction.

Requests for College English Course (For Trial Implementation) (2004) (Abbreviated as *The Requests*) proposed that college English teaching aims to cultivate students' comprehensive competence of using English, especially in listening and speaking abilities that enable them to exchange information effectively in oral and written forms in their future job and social communication. Based on it, EFLT should try to strengthen college students' self-study ability and comprehensive cultural competence to satisfy the demand for economic development and international communication. In *Requests for College English Course*, comprehensive competence is attached much importance. Namely, students should possess language competence, (referring to listening, speaking, reading, writing, and translating), cultural competence, communicative competence and self-study ability. In fact, the comprehensive competence is in accordance with ICC. Furthermore, intercultural communication is listed as one of the main courses of college English for the first time.

From the brief review of the syllabus and documents, we can find that the objective of English teaching is approaching the goal of training students' ICC. *English-teaching Syllabus for English Majors in Higher Institutions* (2000) stated that foreign language talents in the 21st century should be characterized by five advantages (Figure 3.1).

According to the Syllabus, the solid language foundation refers to the language competence, i. e. listening, speaking, reading, writing and translating skills, which are the primary quality of the foreign language talents. The wide

```
                    ┌──────────────────────┐
                    │ Characteristics of the│
                    │  Foreign Language     │
                    │  Talents in 21st Century│
                    └──────────────────────┘
```

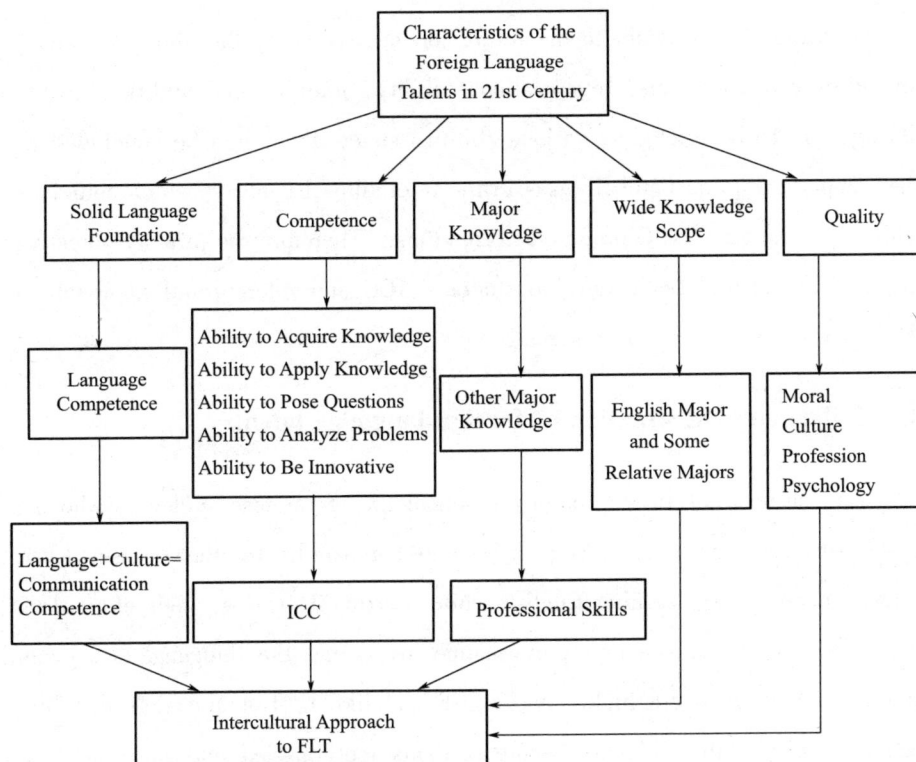

Figure 3. 1　The characteristics of foreign language talents in the 21st century

knowledge scope includes English—major knowledge and the knowledge of some English—related subjects, such as finance, diplomacy. Major knowledge refers to the inter—discipline knowledge which enables the students to work in the fields that have little relation with foreign language. Quality means the requirement of students in moral, culture, profession, physics, and psychology. Competence refers to students' ability to acquire knowledge, apply knowledge, analyze questions, propose ideas independently, and be innovative. In addition, English—major students' ability of applying knowledge is explained as the ability to communicate and cooperate among various cultures, communicative ability, coordinative ability, the ability to adapt to the future job environment, the ability to advise and discuss on problems, organizational ability, interpersonal ability, flexibly ability, etc. To be brief, the various abilities stated above can be concluded as the competence to accomplish tasks in the intercultural context, which coincides with the definition of ICC proposed in this thesis. Therefore the primary objective of our EFLT should be to develop students' ICC and intercultural approach to FLT is designed to achieve this goal.

3. 1. 2 The current situation of foreign language talents

English teaching runs through the school life of Chinese students, who invest most energy and time in English learning compared with other courses. Even a lot of people keep learning English while working. However, their effort does not result in a satisfactory performance of using the language to many students. They can score highly in English test like CET 4 and CET 6. While communicating with foreigners, some students feel puzzled and have no idea about how to start communication. Consequently such nicknames as "dumb English" "deaf English" or "fluent idiot" are used to describe the EFLT in China or Chinese English learners. Traditional FLT in China overemphasizes the training of reading and writing abilities while listening and speaking abilities are not given equal importance. In Denmark, as early as 1995, Aarup Jensen discovered that "language teaching and training have traditionally focused on the cognitive aspect of learning a new language and another culture, whereas the emotional aspects have been underrated in the educational context". In China, college students' competence on behavioral level is neglected in FLT as well.

Wang Zhenya (1990) evaluated the socio-cultural competence of English major students which included three parts: language competence, nonverbal competence and formal culture (referring to the knowledge on politics, geography, history, literature, religion, etc.). The result of the evaluation showed that the subjects' socio-cultural competence is weaker than their language competence and their performance in different components of socio-cultural competence also remains unbalanced, but their verbal competence has a notable advantage over their non-verbal competence, which is a demanding part of ICC for foreign language learners. A similar survey was also conducted by Zhong Hua, Fan Weiwei and Qin Aosong (2001) on non-English major students. Their studies also proved that students' nonverbal competence is not developed equally to their verbal competence. Another discovery of this study is that the students are not skilled in applying the cultural knowledge they have learned in communication.

Gao Yongchen (2006) made a survey of ICC on the English major students of Suzhou University. The result revealed many problems in training students' ICC. 60% of the 257 subjects never read any books related to intercultural communication and knew nothing about this field. For Westerners' habits and customs, nearly half of them chose "know little things about it" and 55.1% chose "know a little" nonverbal knowledge. The worst is that more than one-third of them stated that they have "psychological pressure" and are fearful of communication when answering a foreigner's call for the first time. For the four psychological elements affecting active communication in intercultural interactions: fear for mistakes, introversion, self-abasement, and inferior ICC, 42% chose the last one. Meanwhile, Gao Yong chen made a survey on the ways to improve college students' ICC. For the question "What's the most important problem you meet in intercultural communication?", 58.64% of them chose "lacking the atmosphere for intercultural communication". 43% of students chose "introducing foreign teaching style in the classroom" as the best way to improve their ICC. To some extent, it reflected the students' attitude towards ICC indirectly: it is because their teachers do not create the atmosphere and use foreign teaching styles in class that their ICC is not high. It is completely wrong to neglect teachers' effect in FLT. However, the more profound reason to improve students' ICC lies in the mode and methodology of FLT instead of the teacher.

3. 2 Theoretical foundations

3. 2. 1 The relationship among culture, language and communication

Culture is such a pervasive concept that there have been more than 200 definitions on it. One of the oldest and most quoted definitions of culture was proposed by English anthropologist Edward Burnett Tylor in 1871: "Culture is that complex whole which includes knowledge, belief, art, morals, law, customs and other capabilities and habits acquired by man as a member of society." Kroeber and Kluckhohn (1952) had ever listed 164 definitions of culture that they found in the anthropology literature. From the perspective of FLT, we accept Marsella's conceptualization of culture (1994): "Culture is shared learned behavior which is transmitted from one generation to another for purposes of promoting individual and social survival, adaptation, growth and development. Culture has both external (e. g., artifacts, roles, institutions) and internal representations (e. g., values, attitudes, beliefs, cognitive/affective/ sensory styles, consciousness patterns, and epistemologies)."

Language, as a miracle gift, did great contribution to the development of human being. The famous filmmaker Federico Fellinihas ever used a short sentence to describe the importance of language: "A different language is a different vision of life. " (Nolan, 1999) That is, every language is used as a tool to express people's mind from certain cultural background. And culture is conveyed and reflected by language. Besides, Samovar and Porter (2004) believed that "language serves two important cultural functions. First, it is the means of preserving culture; and second, it is the medium of transmitting culture to new generations. " Therefore, every culture has its unique language, and every language plays a significant role in conveying, protecting and inheriting its culture. On the other hand, as a decisive part of culture, language is influenced by culture which provides resources for language expression. Any language arises and develops in certain cultural background. To conclude, the relationship between language and culture is inseparable. In FLT, it is impossible to isolate language teaching from the teaching of culture. Just as Muller's conclusion (1995), the inclusive relationship that holds between cultural and language makes it necessary for every foreign language lesson to teach, along with the foreign expressions, the foreign culture concepts they convey.

Communication is as difficult to defines as culture. Guoming (1999) defines communication in a reciprocal way: "an interdetermining process in which we develop a mutually dependent relationship by exchanging symbols. " Similarly, Lustig (1999) conceptualized communication as "a symbolic process in which people create shared meanings" . It is worth our attention that symbols in their definitions refer to language, so the meaning conveyed by the symbols should be culturally specific. Whereby communication is actually an interactive process of language and culture. Therefore we regard communication as a process in which the relationship between language and culture is realized. The relationship among language, culture and communication is stated more clearly in Ruben and Stewart's viewpoint: "Human communication is the process through which individuals—in relationships, groups, organizations, and societies—respond to and create messages to adapt to the environment and one another. " (Samovar and Porter, 2004) According to them, messages signify language and environment refers to the cultural context. Based on this thinking, the combination of language teaching and cultural teaching will result in the improvement of students' ICC. That's the objective of intercultural approach to FLT in China.

3. 2. 2 The feature of intercultural communication study

Zhuang Enping (2006) has predicted that cross–discipline study is a trend of academic development in the 21st century. The research of intercultural communication originated from American foreign affairs service in the 1950s. After more than 50 years of development, on the one hand, intercultural communication has been established as an independent discipline with its own theoretical foundation, research methodology, and a lot of achievements. At present, more than 130 universities in the U. S. offer the course of intercultural communication. Some of them provide the MA and Ph. D programs of intercultural communication (ibid). On the other hand, the research of intercultural communication has been absorbed in many other disciplines. Scholars from management, psychology, mass media, etc. have involved themselves in the research of intercultural communication. Picht (1983) called for interdisciplinary studies with an international perspective, i. e. studies that combine foreign language, culture and intercultural communication with, for instance, economics.

In China, many scholars defined intercultural communication as a cross–discipline or multi – discipline study (Hu, 2006; Jia, 2000; Xu, 2006;

Zhuang, 2006). Moreover, Zhuang Enping (2006) has constructed the frame for the development of intercultural communication research (Figure 3. 2).

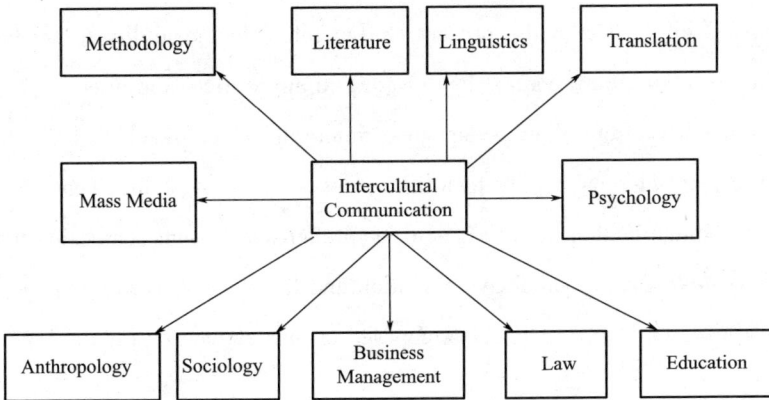

Figure 3. 2 The Frame of Intercultural Communication Development (Zhuang, 2006)

Inferring from Zhuang's framework, we reasonably arrive at the conclusion that the research of intercultural communication can be incorporated with FLT. Then both fields will be broadened and diversified on a large scale. The present study of intercultural approach to FLT serves as an example of such combination.

3. 3 Teaching objectives

According to Zhang Longling (2006), intercultural foreign language teaching has two goals: improving foreign language learners' foreign language communicative competence and improving foreign language learners' intercultural communication competence. In the author's opinion, the two goals are accordant and can be achieved correspondingly in the course of FLT. Therefore intercultural approach to FLT aims to improve students' ICC by means of FLT. Meanwhile, we emphasize that students' ICC is enhanced during the training of language competence, i. e. listening, speaking, reading, writing and translating.

First of all, ICC, in the present study, refers to the ability to accomplish tasks in the intercultural context by engaging in appropriate and effective communication. Different from other pedagogies, intercultural approach to FLT stresses the training of students' ability to fulfilling tasks, instead of language ability or language communication ability. It is a comprehensive system composing four dimensions: mentality, psychology, cognition and behavior. According to Yang and Zhuang's research (2007), ICC is composed of four elements (Figure 3. 3):

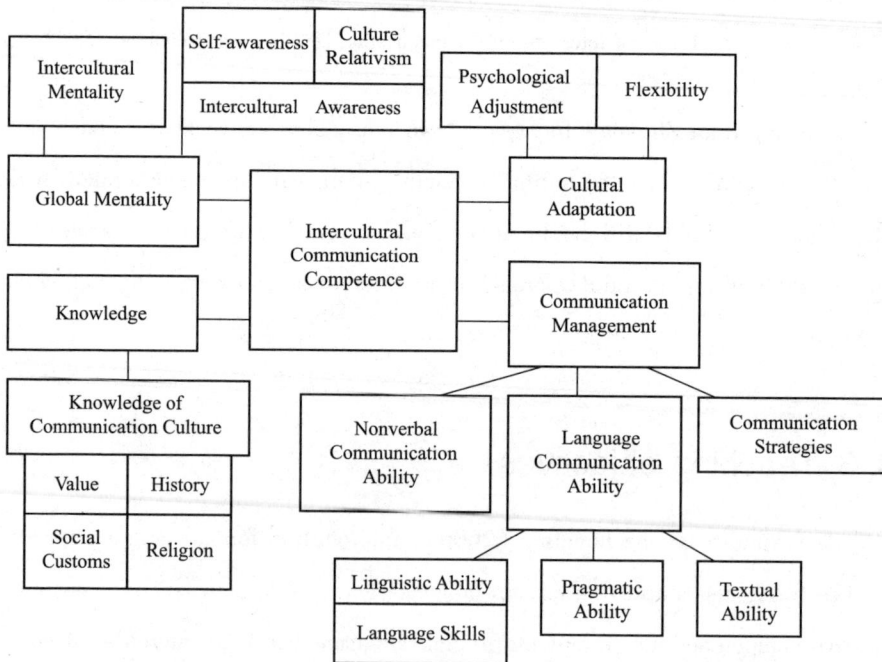

Figure 3. 3   ICC model for EFL teaching (Yang and Zhuang, 2007)

(1) Global mentality: It serves as the foundation of ICC. It consists of two parts: intercultural awareness and intercultural mentality. According to Yang and Zhuang (ibid), intercultural awareness refers to people's understanding of social values, social customs, social norms, and social systems of the native culture and alien culture. Similarly, Lustig (1999) stated: "Individual characteristics and attitudes must be taken into account when trying to understand intercultural competence." Cultural relativism is proposed as opposed to ethnocentrism. It calls for an open mind towards cultural differences and the ability to compre-hend and experience cultural differences (ibid). Intercultural mentality mainly refers to the ability to understand and analyze different cultures. Intercultural understanding is based on the recognition of the differences between cultures (Bredella, 2006). The ability to analyze different cultures requires people to compare, judge, and induce the similarities and differences between cultures (ibid).

(2) Cultural adaptation: It is the requirement of foreign language learners' psychology. It is natural for people who are involved in communication among dif-ferent cultures to suffer from great pressure to their spirit and psychol-ogy. According to Chen and Starosta (1997), the bigger difference between their native culture and the target cultures, the more pressure the communicators will face. Psychological adjustment and flexibility are included in this part. The for-mer refers to the ability to reduce uncertainty and lessen stress and to achieve re-laxation in intercultural interaction. In flexibility, Yang Yin (2007) not only re-ferred to the flexible use of the language but also to the flexible application of in-tercultural knowledge, communication strategies, and so on.

(3) Knowledge: "It is generally assumed that increased knowledge of an-other culture implies increased understanding of ways of thinking and behavior in

the culture in question. And a correct interpretation of a person's behavior pre-supposes knowledge of his or her cultural background. " (Gertsen, 1995) There have been various ways to classify culture. Yang (ibid) adopted a dichotomy of "culture with a capital C" or "high civilization" and "culture with a small c" or "low civilization" (Allen and Valette, 1977; Ovando and Collier, 1985). The former includes human civilizations such as literature, arts, music, architecture, philosophy, and achievements in science and technology. The latter includes customs, lifestyles, social systems, and relationships. On the ground, the knowledge of ICC in FLT mainly refers to "the culture with a small c" .

In addition, the knowledge of one's native culture should never be neglected. Aarup Jensen (1995) likened the culture in which the learner has been raised and educated to the "glasses" through which learners will look at the cultures they meet. Lustig (1999) also said: "knowledge of your own culture will help you to understand another culture" . Therefore, we suggest that both the students' native culture and the culture of the foreign language should be involved in FLT.

(4) Communication management: As the requirement on the behavioral level, it includes language communication ability, nonverbal communication ability, and communication strategies. Language communicative competence comprises language ability, pragmatic ability, and textual ability.

Language ability—the knowledge of a foreign language (e. g. knowledge of pronunciation, lexicon, grammar, structures, meanings, etc.) and its application, namely, five basic language skills—listening, speaking, reading, writing, and translation.

Pragmatic ability—the ability to use appropriate English in social interactions so as to avoid pragmatic failure.

Textual ability—the ability to organize and analyze text both in oral and written forms. Orally, the rules of starting a conversation, taking turns, interrupting, or ending a conversation are culturally bond. In written forms, English texts and Chinese texts are different in structures and rhetoric styles.

Nonverbal competence mainly refers to the ability to apperceive and appropriately use those nonverbal stimuli in intercultural communication settings. According to Samovar (2004), "most classifications divide nonverbal messages into two comprehensive categories: those that are preliminarily produced by the body (appearance, movement, facial expressions, eye contact, touch, smell, and paralanguages); those that the individual combines with the setting (space, time, and silence)."

Strategic competence has been included in communication competence by Canale and Swain (1980) as early as the 1980s. Binon and Claes (1995) analyzed strategic competence on two levels. On the receptive level, strategic competence refers to the ability to "decode the communication strategies and the argumentative strategies of his partners" (ibid). On the productive level, it means the capability of the most adequate strategy in a specific situation (ibid). Hence communication strategy should include the skills to start, maintain, transfer, and end a conversation and the measures to compensate for communication blocks in the intercultural context.

In addition, Yang and Zhuang (2007) drew an inverted pyramid to elaborate on the relationship among the four elements of ICC (Figure 3.4).

According to them, "the four elements of ICC interweave and are interdependent on each other" (ibid). Global mentality serves as the base of ICC. Communication management is the ultimate goal of the other three competencies. It is through communication management that one's preparation in men-

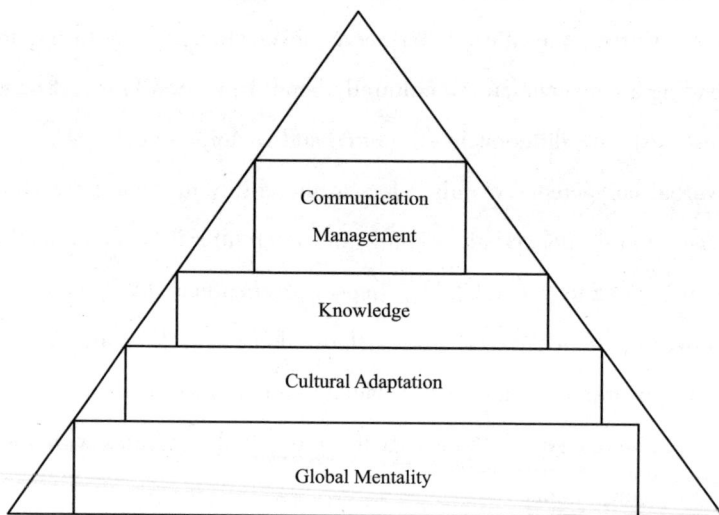

Figure 3. 4   Relationship between four dimensions of ICC (Yang and Wang, 2007)

tality, psychology, and cognition can be transformed in to the ability of accomplishing tasks. Therefore the four elements are integrated and any method to train them separately is wrong.

3. 4 Teaching methods

Once an objective has been defined, it is demanded to choose appropriate teaching methods that facilitate the realization of the teaching objective. Yang and Zhuang (2007) has stated that intercultural FLT, as a teaching mode, takes the form of language teaching and combines awareness development, cultural adaptation training, knowledge teaching, and communication management practice. Based on their viewpoint, I advocate that the training of ICC should be reflected in the teaching of various foreign language courses. ICC can hardly be enhanced if separated from language teaching completely because language qualification is a prerequisite for the students to participate in intercultural activities. In teaching practice, the emphasis varies in the teaching methods of different courses (Figure 3.5).

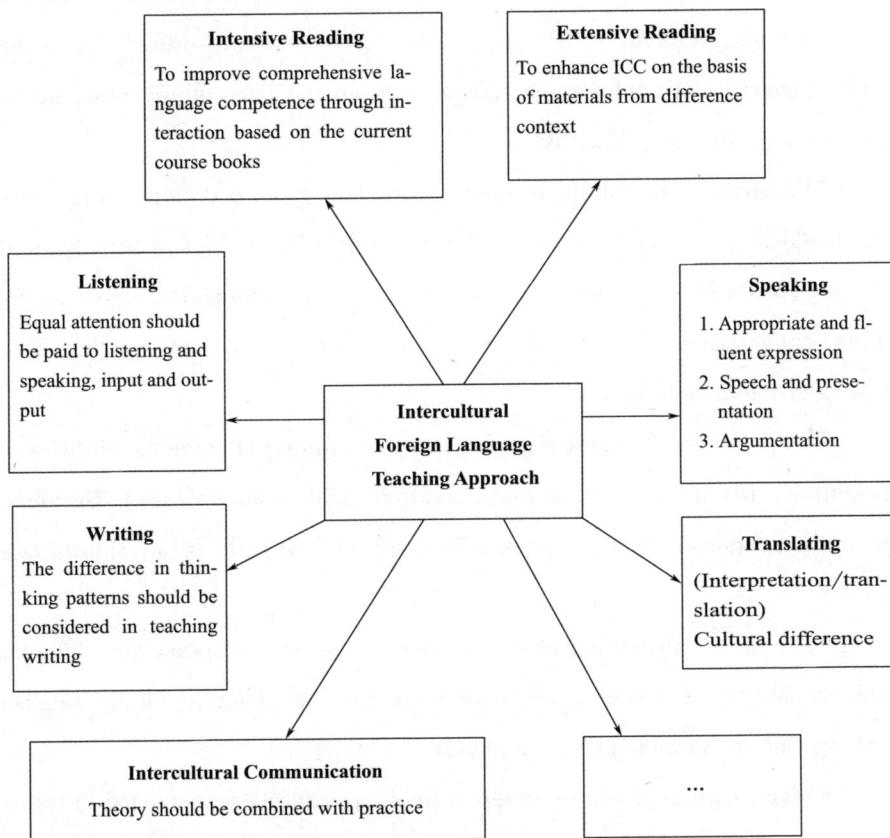

Intensive Reading

To improve comprehensive language competence through interaction based on the current course books

Extensive Reading

To enhance ICC on the basis of materials from difference context

Listening

Equal attention should be paid to listening and speaking, input and output

Speaking

1. Appropriate and fluent expression
2. Speech and presentation
3. Argumentation

Intercultural Foreign Language Teaching Approach

Writing

The difference in thinking patterns should be considered in teaching writing

Translating

(Interpretation/translation)
Cultural difference

Intercultural Communication

Theory should be combined with practice

...

Figure 3. 5   The teaching methods of intercultural approach to FLT

(1) Intensive reading: As a core course of FLT, intensive reading aims to enhance students' comprehensive ability of applying language. In intensive read-

ing class, we stress that students' language competence and ICC should be advanced coincidently in their interaction with various contexts.

(2) Extensive reading: The teaching of extensive reading should be focused on different materials involving various contexts, especially intercultural materials. The selection of texts will be discussed in detail in the next part. By reading these materials, students will be more aware of the cultural differences in the reading material and gradually be able to find out the intercultural problems in texts and real life independently.

(3) Listening: In training listening ability, the input and output of information should be paid equal attention. In other words, the abilities of listening and speaking should be developed mutually. Such forms of information output as retelling, summarizing the material students have listened to, can test the effectiveness of information input.

(4) Speaking: The oral class stresses the training of students' abilities of presenting, persuading, speaking, arguing, and communicating. Besides, the students should learn to speak effectively and fluently in an appropriate context.

(5) Writing: In writing class, various writing styles, especially different thinking patterns in writing, are underlined. Students learn to apply English thinking patterns to their writing gradually.

(6) Translation: Similarly different thinking patterns are reflected in translation as well. Therefore cultural differences should be paid enough attention in both teaching of interpretation and translation.

(7) Intercultural communication: Now many universities have begun to offer the course of intercultural communication. However, in most schools, the teaching of intercultural communication actually aims to introduce the

knowledge of intercultural communication instead of the development of intercultural competence. Considering this situation, we propose that the introduced theories and knowledge should be connected with students' practice in diverse forms, such as case analysis. In the process, students' intercultural knowledge will be transformed to their ability to communicate in intercultural contexts.

(8) There are many other courses in English teaching. In this book, we won't discuss them completely. However, no matter in what courses, two key points should dominate the operating intercultural approach to FLT: various contexts from different cultures and the combination of knowledge and practice.

3. 5 Course books

"Course books are best seen as a resource in achieving the aims and objectives that have already been set in terms of learner needs. " (Cunningsworth, 2002). Thus it is of vital importance that the materials selected for teaching should closely reflect the objective, methods and values of the pedagogy. Recently the author made a survey on the culture–related content in two series of course books widely used in many universities: *An Integrated English Course* (Shanghai Foreign Language Education Press) and *The 21st Century College English* (Fudan University Press and Higher Education Press). It is reflected that there are a certain number of texts concerning a certain culture or intercultural topics, but the quantity is far from being enough to improve the students' ICC. The result of the survey is shown in Table 3. 1.

Table 3. 1 Result of the survey on course books

Name of the Course Books	Amount of the Articles (Four Books)	Amount and Percentage of the Articles Related to a Certain Culture	Amount and Percentage of the Articles Related to Intercultural Contents
An Integrated English Course	128	3/2%	6/4%
The 21st Century College English	96	10/10%	11/11%

The foreign language course book functions as a tool in training foreign language learners' ICC. Figure 3. 6 expounds their relationship. Traditional English course books are mainly composed of two parts: language knowledge and cultural knowledge. The former refers to vocabulary, grammar, structure, etc. The latter is to introduce the cultural background of language. The teaching material and the exercises used in applying intercultural approach to FLT should be based on the construct of ICC (See 3. 3). As Figure 3. 6 illustrates, except the content of traditional course books, intercultural course books should involve intercultural knowledge and practice in various forms. Intercultural knowledge is focused on the comparison of two or more cultures, especially the comparison under the same topic.

Furthermore, practice or exercises are the key step for the students to put what they have learned into use and transform knowledge in to ability on a behavioral level. In the above survey, the author has also found out that most exercises in the course books appear in the objective form, i. e. true or false and multiple choices. Even if there are some thinking questions, they are designed to test students' understanding of the texts' meaning. Students can find out the correct answers directly in the text with no effort. However, without the process of think-

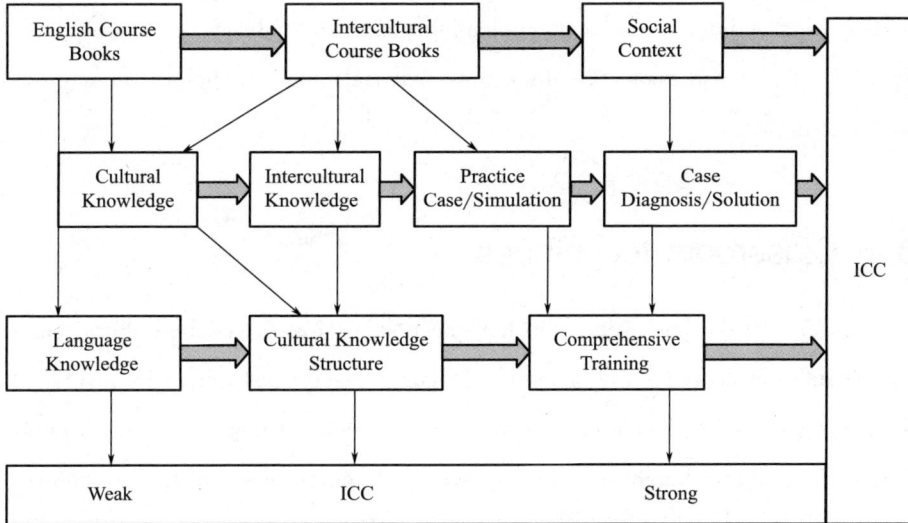

Figure 3. 6   Relationship between ICC and Course Books

ing independently and expressing their ideas with language, students can hardly practice their speaking ability, let alone the improvement of ICC. In addition, culture is a complex subject that can not be easily judged as right or wrong, good or bad. From this perspective, the exercise of true or false will mislead the students to a cultural stereotype. Therefore the ICC oriented exercises in intercultural course books should aim to enhance students' language competence and ICC in various contexts (for instance, the cases reflecting intercultural conflicts which can be used to encourage students' discussion and presentation).

Social context where communication happens naturally is the optimum environment for the training of ICC. However, classroom teaching can hardly exert the same effectiveness as the practice in social context. Thus some exercises can be designed to motivate students' attention to the intercultural problems in their life. The training in class will enable the students to diagnose the problem and find out the resolution independently, which will lay a hard base for students participating in intercultural communication activities. In brief, as a useful tool for FLT, the course books should supply materials that are helpful to improve students' ICC.

3. 6 Classroom techniques

Jæger (1995) has ever posed the question: "How to get the cultural component into the everyday life of foreign language teaching at university level?" I think the answer lies in the classroom teaching of foreign language, which determines the accomplishment of teaching tasks and achievements of teaching objectives. From the ICC model in FLT, it is inferred that the training of ICC should abide by the sequence: contacting → understanding → analysis → practice. Accordingly, Yang (2007) proposed five classroom techniques to coordinate the FLT at different stages: introducing cultural background, exploring cultural information of language, case analysis, role−play and simulation, and case diagnosis and resolution. Meanwhile, she made a model for intercultural EFL teaching, based on which we construct the classroom teaching process of intercultural approach to FLT (Figure 3.7). The details of each technique are elaborated in the model.

3. 6. 1 Introducing cultural background

Cultural background refers to the background knowledge concerning the language materials. It is one of the widely−employed techniques in cultural teaching nowadays. Background knowledge not only helps to increase students' cultural accumulation and cultural awareness, but also enriches the teaching resources. Thus

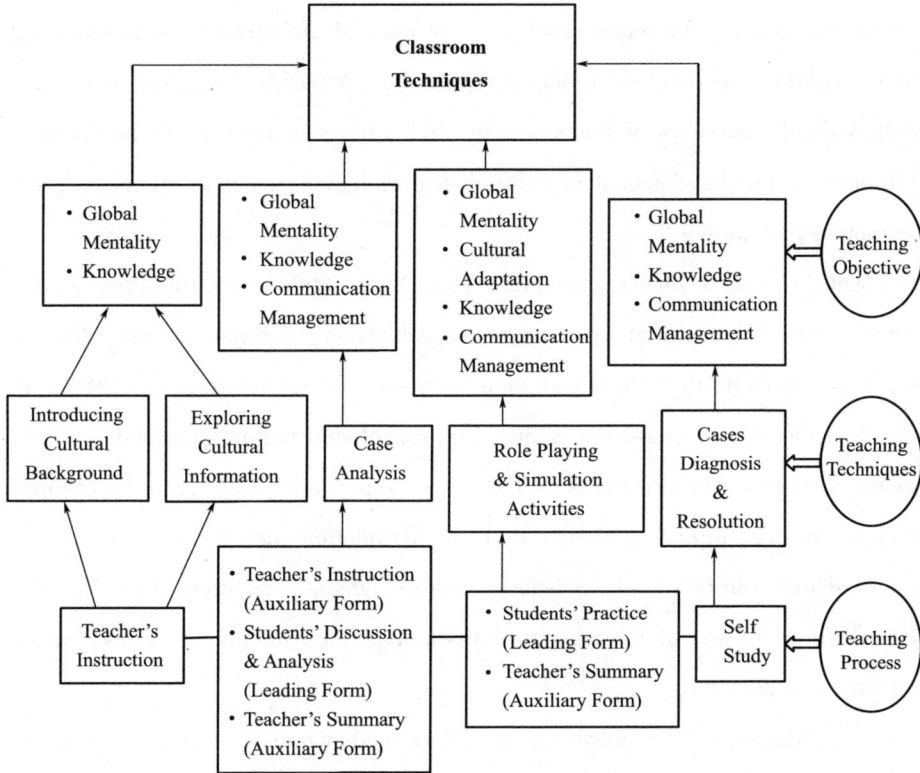

Figure 3. 7   A Model of classroom techniques for Intercultural approach to FLT

it is very popular in college English teaching to train students' ICC. However, the result of its application is not satisfactory, because foreign language teachers seldom understand the theory of cultural teaching. Introducing cultural background does not mean to reduplicate the knowledge of foreign cultures simply. Some principles are necessary for effective introduction. Zhao Houxian (2002) has put forward four cultural teaching principles in English teaching: cognitive principle, absorptive principle, comparative principle and tolerant principle. Cognitive principle refers to the students' knowledge acquisition of the target culture through teachers' introduction. Absorptive principle is to absorb what is favorable to native culture from the target culture and refine and assimilate them to serve the native culture. Comparative principle means the comparison of native and target cultures and awareness of the similarity and difference between them. Tolerant principle is the abandonment of cultural discrimination, such as ethnocentrism, stereotype, prejudice.

On the basis of Zhao's principles, Yang Ying (2007) proposed three guidelines of inserting cultural elements: comprehension, correlation, and diversity. In her opinion, the rule of comprehension calls for intercultural understanding which is the core of knowledge acquisition. Correlation requires that cultural elements inserted in the process of FLT must be helpful and practical to the training of ICC. In intercultural approach to FLT, correlation also means the cultural knowledge should be closely associated with the language material. Diversity indicates various means of inserting or introducing, for example, lectures, newspapers, videos, etc.

In addition, what to introduce in FLT is another important problem faced by foreign language teachers. In traditional FLT, political or historical facts of another culture are frequently chosen as cultural knowledge to compensate language teaching. However, in terms of practicability, these kinds of knowledge have low frequency of use in students' daily life. The knowledge imparted should be centered on the culture in life that can be grasped and made use of easily in students' communication activities.

According to Figure 3.7, introducing cultural background is used in the initial stage of a foreign language class. From the perspective of the ICC model (see Figure 3.3), the technique aims to increase students' global mentality and knowledge. Teachers play the leading role in using the technique.

3. 6. 2 Exploring cultural information in language

Cultural information refers to the cultural connotation hidden in language components, such as grammar, lexicon, text, etc. The close relation between culture and language makes cultural information exploration necessary and important to cultural teaching. Whorf (1956) has ever concluded that grammar influences people's perception of the worldby analyzing the language of Hopi. Hence in grammar teaching, teachers should try to discover the difference in tense, word order, sentence structure, etc. in different languages, compare them and find out their cultural origins. Lexicon carries abundant cultural information. In teaching vocabulary, teachers should pay as much attention to the social and historical factors hidden in them as to their meaning. The text in language teaching appears in two kinds of forms: oral text and written text. With regard to the oral text, communication styles and strategies that are culturally – bound should be emphasized. While analyzing the written text, the exploration of culture can be focused on the discourse style. Kaplan (1966) has drawn five diagrams to symbolize various cultural thought patterns that manifest the discourse features of different languages. According to him, English speakers usually organize the text in a "linear" way, while Chinese people are accustomed to a round or spiral way. Based on this, teachers can compare the articles written by English people and Chinese writers on the same topic and elaborate the different thought patterns reflected by their language.

Similar to introducing cultural background, this technique is used at the preliminary stage of teaching with the aim of strengthening students' global mentality and knowledge. Also, it should be the teachers who decide what to explore and how to present them to the students in an acceptable way.

3. 6. 3 Case study

Case-teaching method originated from MBA program of Business School in Harford. Since 1908 when the Business School was established in Harford, it has been spread to the teaching of many other fields, such as law, medical science (Chen, 2004). At present, it is widely used in FLT. Chen Jianping (ibid) defined the case in FLT as the description of the real situation which requires students' thinking, analysis and absorption. In intercultural approach to FLT, case study aims to teach the students how to analyze a case from an intercultural perspective and solve the intercultural problems in the cases.

We give the priority to the case selection. On the one hand, the complex intercultural questions or conflicts should be conveyed by the cases that will evoke students' thinking and discussion. On the other hand, cases in this part should be famous events or incidents involving intercultural problems that are convincing and persuading. The form can be various, such as misunderstanding in transnational marriages, cultural conflicts in the film *Guasha*, the intercultural problem caused by companies' merger, for instance Lenovo and the PC of IBM. They provide valuable materials for students' analysis of intercultural activities. In addition, case study should be conducted in certain orders. Chen (ibid) proposed four steps in applying cases: preparation, analysis and discussion, conclusion, and writing report. Here we adopt Yang Ying (2007) 's five steps listed for case analysis. They are pre-reading questions, case reading, case analysis, group discussion, and teacher's conclusion and comments. Pre-reading questions offer the students some hints about the topic of language materials. Case reading is the comprehension phase which trains the students' reading skills and the ability to find out effective cultural information while reading. Case analysis is a process to teach students how to think, estimate, and judge facts from an intercultural per-spective. It is significant to train students' intercultural awareness. In group dis-cussion, students talk and exchange their ideas with each other, through which both their language abilities and communication skills are improved. Last, case study should be concluded by the teachers. Teachers' summary and comments will serve as the guarantee to the efficacy of students' activities.

The cases should be used in the middle stage of a class as an auxiliary to the language material. Except the training on mentality and knowledge level, case study involves students' practice on a behavioral level—communication management (See Figure 3. 3). In this procedure, students act as the leading role in the classroom. Teachers' function is mainly reflected in encouraging students' participation and instructing and commenting on students' discussions.

3. 6. 4 Role-plays and simulations

As early as 1976, Paulston & Bruder defined role – play as "exercises where the student is assigned a fictitious role from which he was to improvise some kind of behavior toward the other role characters in the exercise". Jane Revell (1983) thought "role-play could be defined as an individual's spontane-ous behavior reacting to others in a hypothetical situation". Littlewood (1981) listed six kinds of role-play and simulation activities: role-playing controlled through cued dialogue, role-playing controlled through cures and information, role-playing controlled through situation and goals, role-playing in the form of debate or discussion, large-scale situation activities, and improvisation. From Littlewood's viewpoint, role-play and simulation are closely related. "All role-play activities involve simulation, but differ in terms of teacher – control and learner-creativity" (ibid).

In intercultural approach to FLT, both role—play and simulation are processes in which students take certain roles in the emulated situations to actively experience the nature of life in another culture by acting, discussing and interpreting situations. Accordingly, three key parts are concluded: the context or situation, the roles and language expression. First of all, both role—plays and simulations are highly culture—specific (Gertsen, 1995). Thus the situation chosen should be representative of the communicative contexts in real life so that the students can obtain more direct and useful experience from their practice. Meanwhile "the situation must be capable of stimulating learners to a high degree of communicative involvement" (ibid). Secondly, the role should be assigned to the students appropriately and reasonably. Students' personal factors, such as their characteristics, language skill, should be taken into consideration. Alternatively students can select the role independently with the teachers' instruction. Last but not least, fluent expression functions as a tool which decides the effectiveness of the activity. To guarantee the quality of the activity, teachers should ensure students share adequate knowledge.

Role—play and simulation activities aim at improving students' ICC through their own experience and feelings in the simulated communicative situations. Thus students' leading roles must be confirmed. But their activities should be under specific instructions and control. Therefore, teachers' job will be more concerned in the controlling of preparation, organization, control, and summary of the activity. This technique should be used at the concluding stage of a class to help students strengthen the knowledge and skills acquired at the previous stages. Because it has higher requirements of students' language skill, it usually is adopted in the advanced training of ICC. In the process of activities, students' ICC on the four levels is put into practice on a full scale, especially their global mentality and communication management competence.

3. 6. 5 Case diagnosis and resolution

Only by being put to use, can every knowledge or skill be really acquired by the learners and transformed to learners' competence. Therefore, in order to train ICC, a lot of opportunities should be provided to students who will be able to use what they have learned in class to solve problems in intercultural communications happening in their lives. Since the time in class is limited, a large amount of training should be conducted after class. Case diagnosis and resolution are designed to fulfill the function. Different from the classical cases used in case studies, the cases are not necessarily very famous and influential, but it is of vital importance that they involve cultural conflicts or communicative problems which will inspire students' thinking and practice. Teachers should inspire their students to observe the communications around them through various channels: media, survey, interview, intern, etc. Gradually students are able to analyze them from an intercultural perspective, find out the intercultural problem hidden in the communications, and finally solve the problems with their knowledge and skills obtained in class independently. Possibly this activity can be fulfilled by a group. Members should cooperate to cope with the intercultural problems in their study or work. Through this practice, the student will possess the ability to accomplish their tasks in the intercultural context which conforms to the Syllabus' requirements of foreign language talents of the 21st century. It is the objective of intercultural approach to FLT as well.

Different from the above techniques, case diagnosis and resolution are usually conducted after class. Accordingly, students in the process mainly depend on themselves to find problems in the cases and solve them. But they still need to report or present their experience as the feedbacks which should be commented on and summarized by teachers.

In conclusion, every technique has its unique function and serves a certain stage of FLT. Whereas, all of them are characterized by task- based or problem-solving based teaching. In other words, the teaching objective of intercultural approach to FLT can be achieved mainly by students' involvement in series of activities which are designed and organized to guide their solving problems and fulfilling tasks in teaching various kinds of foreign language courses. Therefore students' classroom participation under the teachers' effective organization is emphasized. In this way, not only will students' understanding of the text be deepened, but also their abilities to think and express independently will be strengthened.

3. 7 Teachers

Different teaching methods pose different demands and responsibilities to teachers. In the grammar–translation methods, teachers are required to " know the target language and its literature thoroughly, but do not necessarily speak the language fluently" (Dubin and Olshtain, 2002). Audio–lingual method demands language teachers to " be the native speaker of the target language" (ibid). In implementing intercultural approach to FLT, the teacher is more like a controller, because the approach advocates students' participation under the teachers' effective organization and guide, which is a big challenge to teachers' overall qualification. In addition to their specialized knowledge, teachers employing intercultural approach to FLT should be good at designing, organizing, and guiding class activities. However, the status quo of our English teachers is far from satisfying the requirement. Dai Weidong (2001) investigated the English teachers' quality and found that Chinese English teachers' quality, professional level, and teaching investment, i. e. the energy and time invested in teaching, are not satisfying. Among the 282 subject teachers, nearly half of them thought FLT in their regions was suffering from the deficiency of qualified foreign language teachers. Therefore, it is of high necessity to conduct the training for teachers who will apply intercultural approach to FLT in their teaching. The training is mainly concerned with four perspectives: the system of intercultural approach to FLT, the research of intercultural communication, the research of ICC, and flexibility in classroom teaching.

(1) The system of intercultural approach to FLT: Dai Weidong and Ren Qingmei (2007) pointed out that the teachers who don't understand the theoretical background of teaching and learning can never teach effectively. Therefore, to a teacher who will use intercultural approach to FLT, it is a basic qualification to study and understand its system thoroughly including its theoretical foundation, objectives, methods, etc.

(2) The intercultural communication research: As a new discipline, intercultural communication is unfamiliar to many English teachers. Since intercultural approach to FLT is established on the basis of theories and achievements of intercultural communication study, being acquainted with the discipline of intercultural communication is helpful to teachers' understanding and application of the approach.

(3) ICC: Intercultural approach to FLT ICC is to improve foreign language learners' ICC. Thus it is essential for foreign language teachers to understand the definition of ICC correctly. Meanwhile, teachers should try to enhance their own ICC. To some extent, their degree of ICC determines the degree of effectiveness

of the approach in their teaching.

(4) Flexibility in classroom teaching: Although intercultural approach to FLT emphasizes students' involvement, it doesn't mean any neglect of teachers' role. On the contrary, it poses greater challenges to teachers' comprehensive qualifications. Whether students will take an active part in the classroom activities and whether their ICC can be improved during the participation depend on the teachers' flexibility in the classroom teaching on a large scale.

Chapter 4　An Experimental Application
of Intercultural Approach to FLT
in the Classroom

The value of any method or approach is determined by its effectiveness in teaching practice. Therefore in the study, it is a key issue to know if intercultural approach to FLT can improve foreign language learners' ICC effectively in class-room teaching. With this regard, the author conduct the pedagogical experiment in which intercultural approach is tried in the FLT classroom of some college students. After four-month experiment, the students' ICC will be compared with that of those who are taught in a non-experiment class. By doing so, the author hopes to obtain some information for future study.

Intercultural approach to FLT in China is a complicated system whose effec-tiveness can be proved by the full employment of intercultural approach to FLT in classroom teaching. Compared with the whole system, the teaching techniques of intercultural approach to FLT are more specific and can exert their effectiveness more easily and directly. Therefore in the present study, the experiment is con-ducted mainly to prove if the teaching techniques are effective in improving students' ICC in FLT. To some extent, the result of the empirical study will sup-ply some support for the further study of intercultural approach to FLT.

4. 1 Preparation

52 English-major freshmen from two classes and 70 non-English-major sophomores from two classes are sampled at random as the subjects. The participants are enrolled at Shanghai University in September 2007 and 2006. There is no marked difference in language competence based on their scores on entrance examination. Besides, only five of them (4% of the total subjects) expressed that they have ever taken the course of intercultural communication and nine (6% of the total subjects) indicated that they have a chance to communicate with foreigners frequently. Therefore the majority of the participants have never taken any course of intercultural communication and no marked difference is discovered in their ICC.

In the study, students of English majors (Class 1 and Class 2) are named as English group (EG) and non-English group (NEG) includes students of Class 3 and Class 4. In both groups, Class 1 and Class 3 are chosen as the experiment classes while the other two classes are the control classes. The information of the subjects is provided in Table 4. 1 and Table 4. 2.

Table 4. 1 Information of EG

Items	The Experiment Class (Class 1)	The Control Class (Class 2)
Number of Students	28	24
Average Age	19	19
Proportion between Male and Female Students	7. 1% (Male) 92. 9% (Female)	20. 8% (Male) 79. 2% (Female)
Average Year of English Study	10. 18	10. 21

Table 4. 2 Information of NEG

Items	The Experiment Class (Class 3)	The Control Class (Class 4)
Number of Students	31	39
Average Age	20	20
Proportion between Male and Female Students	41. 9% (Male) 58. 1% (Female)	15. 4% (Male) 84. 6% (Female)
Average Year of English Study	11. 29	11. 30

The teaching material used in the experiment is provided by author of this book and the course books: *College English Intensive Reading <1>* (Foreign Language Press) to EG and *A New English Course (Revised edition)* (Shanghai Foreign Language Education Press) to NEG. The material the author selected covers four parts: background information, cultural notes, case analysis, and role-play, all of which are closely related to the theme of each unit. The former two parts focus on an introduction of the cultural values and they are designed in accordance with the first two teaching techniques proposed above, while the latter two activities are designed to improve students' ICC on behavioral dimension. In addition, multimedia equipments are available during the teaching process.

The experiment was executed by the author's supervisor in Class 1 and by other teachers in the rest classes.

4. 2 Procedure

During the four months, the teaching was carried out in a normal order. Class 1 and Class 3 were lectured by using the five techniques of intercultural approach to FLT. Based on knowledge introduction, the teachers encouraged students to participate in some ICC-oriented activities, such as discussion, presentation, role-play. In addition to the course books, many cases and events on intercultural communication were added in various ways. While teachers of the control classes mainly used traditional teaching models. The class was focused on explaining grammar, sentence, meaning, etc. and the training of speaking ability was emphasized in the classroom practice. Non-ICC-oriented activities were organized for the control classes.

4.3 Data collection

At the end of the experiment, a questionnaire designed by Yang Ying is employed to test the subjects' ICC. It is composed of 39 items mainly testing people's ICC from three perspectives: knowledge orientation, attitude/awareness, and adaptation in intercultural communication context. As Table 4.3 displays, 6 items in the questionnaire are designed to test if the subjects know the knowledge

Table 4.3 Distribution of the questionnaire (Yang, 2007)

Items			Number	
Knowledge Orientation			6	
Attitude/Awareness			7	
Adaptation in IC Context	Behavioral Adjustment According to Value Differences	High/Low Context	5	26
		Individualism/Collectivism	3	
		Uncertainty Avoidance	3	
		Power Distance	3	
		Masculinity/Femininity	1	
		Time Orientation	1	
	Nonverbal Communication		3	
	Communication Styles and Strategies		5	
	Stress		2	

used in intercultural communication. However, the majority of the questions are concerned with people's adaptation in intercultural communication contexts, i. e. what are their attitudes towards the cultural difference in various contexts? How will they deal with the intercultural problems in their lives? Hence the questionnaire will mainly reflect the testees' ICC from a behavioral perspective. The reliability and validity of the items have been testified by Yang Ying. After data collection, the statistical program SPSS (Statistical Package for Social Science 11. 0) for Windows is utilized for the quantitative analysis of the data.

4. 4 Data analysis

4. 4. 1 Mean score

The total score of the questionnaire is 153, which is 32. 25 percent higher than the mean score of the total subjects (103. 65). It implies that the current status of the students' ICC is not satisfying. Figure 4. 1 displays the mean score of EG. The experiment class in EG (Class 1) scores 108. 32, which is almost 3 percent higher than the mean of the control class of the group (104. 63). Similarly in NEG, Class 3's mean score (103. 87) is 4 percent higher than that of Class 4 (99. 51) (Figure 4. 2). Generally speaking, the experiment classes do better in the survey than the control classes in both EG and NEG.

4. 4. 2 T-test

To analyze the effectiveness of intercultural approach to FLT further, Inde-

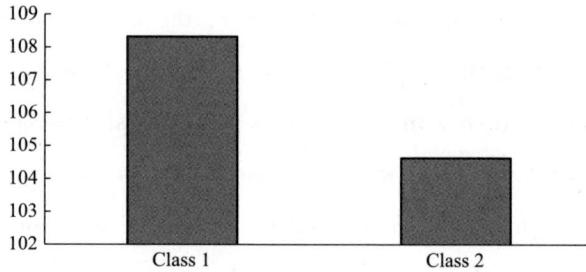

Figure 4. 1　Mean of EG

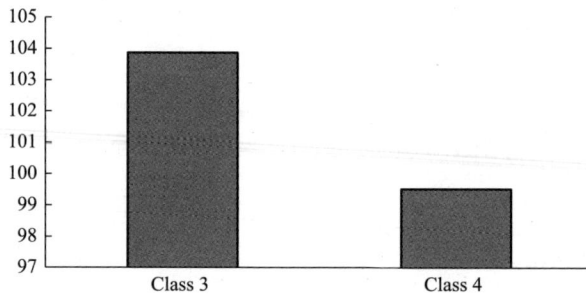

Figure 4. 2　Mean of NEG

pendent-Samples T test is also conducted in both groups. The results are shown in Table 4. 4 and Table 4. 5 respectively.

　　Table 4. 4 shows that the T value of the test within EG is 0. 044 ($t=0. 05$), and according to Table 4. 5, the T value within NEG is 0. 042 ($t=0. 05$). Both values are lower than the standard T value 0. 05. That is to say, significant difference of ICC exists between the experiment class and the control class of both groups. Therefore it can be concluded that through four months' application of intercultural approach to FLT to teaching practice, the experiment classes perform better in ICC than the control classes. Accordingly, intercultural approach to FLT is effective to improve students' ICC during the course of FLT.

Table 4. 4   Result of T-test within EG

Items	Levene's Test for Quality of Variance		T-test for Equality of Means						
	F	Sig.	*t*	*df*	Sig. (2-tailed)	Mean Difference	Std. Error Difference	95% Confidence Interval of the Difference	
								Lower	Upper
ICC Equal Variances Assumed	0	0. 987	2. 068	50	0. 044	4. 7381	2. 29116	0. 13616	9. 34003
ICC Equal Variances Non-Assumed			2. 072	49. 095	0. 044	4. 7381	2. 28727	0. 14188	9. 33431

F: used to test whether the variances of the two samples are equal.

Sig. : represent the significance level of the homogeneity of variance test.

T: used to test whether the means of the two samples are equal.

df: degrees of freedom, is the number of independent pieces of information used to calculate a statistic.

Sig. (2-tailed): The "Sig" entry in the output for independent samples is the two-tailed p-value for the null hypothesis that the two groups have the same variances.

Table 4. 5   Result of T-test within NEG

Items	Levene's Test for Quality of Variance		T-test for Equality of Means						
	F	Sig.	*t*	*df*	Sig. (2-tailed)	Mean Difference	Std. Error Difference	95% Confidence Interval of the Difference	
								Lower	Upper
ICC Equal Variances Assumed	0. 227	0. 635	2. 101	68	0. 039	4. 6807	2. 22811	0. 23460	9. 12686
ICC Equal Variances Non-Assumed			2. 079	61. 620	0. 042	4. 6807	2. 25141	0. 17968	9. 18178

Annotations are the same as Table 4. 4.

4. 5 Results and discussion

After four months of experiment, the experiment classes' ICC is higher than that of the control classes on average (Figure 4. 1). Besides, Figure 4. 2 indicates that in terms of intercultural attitude, the experiment class scores higher than the control class by 4 percent in the EG and 2 percent in the NEG. To the dimension of adaptation in IC context, the degrees of difference between the experiment class and the control class of EG and NEG are both almost 3 percent. The results of T-test (Table 4. 4 and Table 4. 5) also prove that there are significant differences of ICC between the experiment class and the control class in both groups. Therefore it can be concluded that intercultural approach to FLT is effective in improving foreign language learners' ICC in the course of FLT.

Meanwhile, the author find out that the college students' ICC is far from being satisfying, especially on the behavioral dimension of ICC. In the questionnaire, to question No. 25 "I am fluent in foreign language, but in communicating with foreigners, I feel nervous and scared", 69 students which covers 56. 6 percent of the total chose "most of the time". Besides 73 students, 59. 5 percent of the whole subjects, chose "agree" in answering question No. 27 "I'm willing to communicate with foreigners, but I don't know how to avoid misunderstanding in communicating with them". Therefore improving college students' ICC on the behavioral dimension should be emphasized for future research on intercultural approach to FLT.

Although a large amount of time and energy has been devoted to the study, several limitations should be mentioned. Firstly, the number of samples is not large enough, and the subjects are all from one university, which are not so representative of the college students all over the country. Greater samples of college students representing universities of different geological locations and academic standards are recommended in future studies. Secondly, the study is conducted within a limited time. Although differences have been testified between the treatment classes and the control classes, more correct and ideal results will be arrived at for a longer time experiment.

4. 6 Conclusion

The part is a preliminary study of intercultural approach to FLT in China. The author attempts to build the system of the approach and prove that it is effective to improve college students' ICC in FLT.

Intercultural approach to FLT is proposed on two theoretical foundations. On the one hand, the interrelationship awong language, culture, and communication provides the possibility. On the other hand, the study of intercultural communication is characterized by inter-discipline, which guarantees the feasibility of the approach. Intercultural approach to FLT aims to improve students' ICC during FLT. ICC is a holistic system consisting of four dimensions: global mentality, cultural adaptation, knowledge, and communication management. Of the whole system of ICC, communication management is the core in which people's preparations in the other three aspects are realized.

It is a misunderstanding to separate FLT from the training of ICC. On the contrary, ICC development should be reflected in the teaching of foreign language courses. Thus different methods are designed to realize intercultural approach to FLT in the teaching of different courses, such as intensive reading, translation, writing. Besides present course books are to be improved to operate intercultural approach in teaching. Based on the traditional course book, intercultural knowledge should be included in the intercultural course book. Various forms of exercises and practices such as case analysis and simulation activities are suggested to be added.

In order to achieve the goal of intercultural approach to FLT better, five techniques are put forward to guide classroom teaching of FLT: introducing cultural background, exploring cultural information, case analysis, role-play and simulation activities, and case diagnosis and resolution. Each technique is proposed to be used in a certain period of teaching.

A teacher is an organizer and executor of effective teaching. As an advanced teaching theory, intercultural approach to FLT demands foreign language teachers having higher qualifications. Considering that the approach emphasizes students' participation in teaching, teachers who will apply intercultural approach to FLT are required to accept the training of the four aspects: the system of intercultural approach to FLT, the research of intercultural communication, the research of ICC, and flexibility in classroom teaching.

Last but not least, intercultural approach to FLT is applied to classroom teaching to testify its effectiveness. 122 college students who are divided into two groups (EG and NEG) are involved in the experiment. The techniques are applied to the English teaching of the experiment classes in both groups. After four months experiment, the questionnaire designed by Yang Ying (2007) is adopted to test the subjects' ICC. The data are processed with the statistical program SPSS. By comparing the results of the two kinds of classes, it is discovered that in both EG group and NEG, the ICC of the experiment class is higher than that of the control class and the difference was significant. In other words, intercultural approach to FLT is effective to improve students' ICC. Meanwhile, the quantitative analysis reveals that the status quo of college students' ICC is not satisfying, especially on the behavioral level. College students are not competent enough to solve the problems they will meet in intercultural communication. Therefore enhancing college students' ICC in an all-around way should be an emphasis of FLT reform.

Chapter 5   Challenges of Intercultural
Approach to FLT in the Digital Time

5. 1 Introduction

At the end of 2019, the pandemic of COVID – 19 confronted the online teaching in colleges with anunprecedented challenge. According to *Chinese Education Daily*, "By May 8th, 2023, 1454 colleges have used online teaching, 1. 03 million college teachers opened 1. 07 million courses, and 17. 75 million college students studied online. " At the beginning of 2020, the virus spread fast in America. Some mainstream media like *Washington Post* have commented that COVID–19 made American education experience a historic and perpetual revolution. The data of *Education Weekly* showed that more than 120 thousand schools and education institutions closed and changed to online teaching mode urgently since the pandemic broke out. In order to improve the communication in information technology–based teaching between the two countries, Shandong Vocational College of Light Industry and Mississippi College cooperated to make research aiming to grasp the status quo and problems in the online teaching of the two countries and provide constructive suggestions.

5. 2 Methodology

5. 2. 1 Participants

Participants in the study were 465 volunteers out of 700 college students and teachers participating in the online courses during the pandemic in Mississippi, and 711 volunteers out of 1000 in Shandong. It resulted in a volunteer rate of 66. 43% for Mississippi and 71. 10% for Shandong. They came from 17 colleges of Mississippi State and 20 colleges of Shandong Province. Table 5. 1 shows the details of the volunteers enrolled in the study. Meanwhile, 108 of the participants were chosen to take interview at random. Table 5. 2 shows the details of the interview participants.

Table 5. 1 Details of participants

Items		China (711, 60. 46%)		America (465, 39. 54%)	
		Students	Teachers	Students	Teachers
Gender	Male	213 (45. 13%)	131 (54. 81%)	144 (47. 84%)	89 (54. 27%)
	Female	259 (54. 87%)	108 (45. 19%)	157 (52. 16%)	75 (45. 73%)
Average Age		20. 13	47. 13	21. 45	43. 54

Table 5. 2 Interview participants

Items		China (62, 57. 41%)		America (46, 42. 59%)	
		Students	Teachers	Students	Teachers
Gender	Male	15 (40. 54%)	11 (44. 00%)	10 (35. 71%)	7 (38. 89%)
	Female	22 (59. 46%)	14 (56. 00%)	18 (64. 29%)	11 (61. 11%)
Average Age		19. 98	45. 46	20. 25	45. 67

5. 2. 2 Questionnaire

The questionnaire is designed from four perspectives: teaching mode, course sources, platform and technology, effectiveness, and satisfaction. The interview is taken by means of social media, phone calls, and text messages.

5. 3 Results

5. 3. 1 Teaching mode

With the outbreak of virus, colleges and universities of both countries transformed the blending teaching mode to online teaching. Zoom was used in online teaching besides the previously used online course platform.

Most Chinese college teachers used Excellent Course Platform, Excellent Shared Course Platform, Massive Open Online Course Platform, etc. to upload resources, organize teaching, and evaluate teaching effectiveness. Meanwhile, online meeting APPs, like Zoom, Ding Talk, and VooV Meeting, are frequently used to proceed real-time teaching.

In the United States, most college teachers in the study used more fragmented teaching materials that were created and accumulated in their daily teaching, instead of constructed and systematic online courses. In Mississippi College, MOODLE is the key Platform to assist teaching, in which teachers carried out most major activities as uploading materials, assigning tasks, testing and grading, communicating with students, etc. In real-time teaching, Zoom is the most frequently used APP by college teachers.

5. 3. 2 Course resource

As for the variety of teaching resources, 7 types of online resources are listed by the college teachers and students of both countries. They are video, audio, text (including Power Point), App, educational website, E-book, and three-dimensional animation. They are ranked according to the using quantity and frequency, whose result is shown in Figure 5. 1. Text resource is used most by the students of both countries, but Chinese students use 13% more than American students. Meanwhile, the different kinds of resources are distributed more uniform in American students. Comparing with them, Chinese students' result shows more divergence, in which text covers absolute majority, while E-book and three-dimensional (3D) animation cover less than 4%. Besides, audio material only used in language-related courses covers least in both countries.

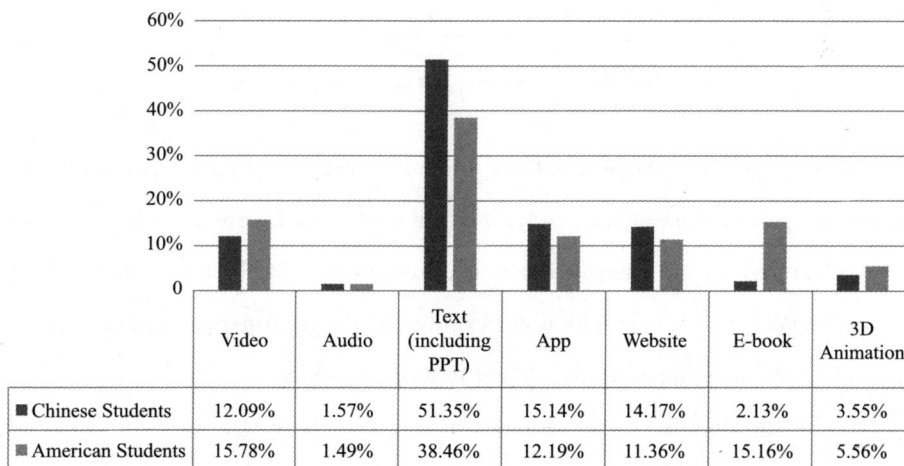

	Video	Audio	Text (including PPT)	App	Website	E-book	3D Animation
■ Chinese Students	12.09%	1.57%	51.35%	15.14%	14.17%	2.13%	3.55%
■ American Students	15.78%	1.49%	38.46%	12.19%	11.36%	15.16%	5.56%

Figure 5. 1 Online teaching resources used by students

The result of college teacher's research (Figure 5. 2) shows that text has the priority among different teaching materials. Similar to the result of students research, American teachers use the resources in a more even way, while Chinese teachers have more disparity.

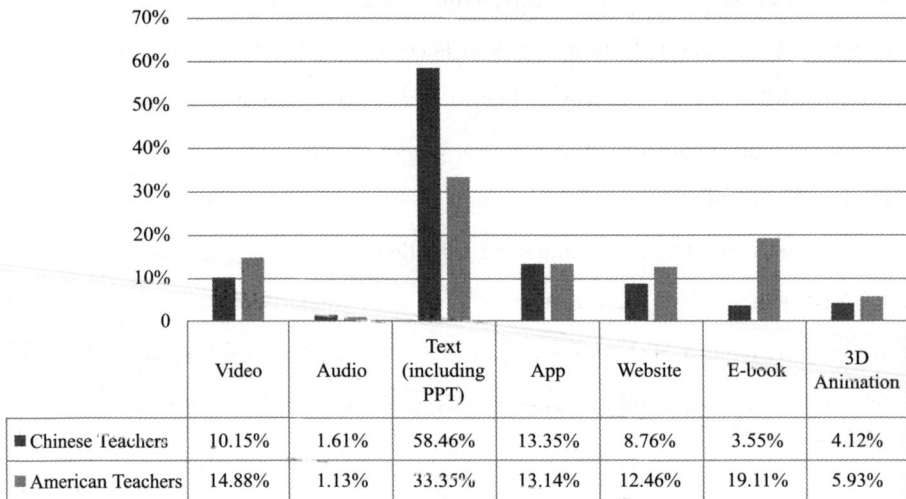

	Video	Audio	Text (including PPT)	App	Website	E-book	3D Animation
■ Chinese Teachers	10.15%	1.61%	58.46%	13.35%	8.76%	3.55%	4.12%
■ American Teachers	14.88%	1.13%	33.35%	13.14%	12.46%	19.11%	5.93%

Figure 5. 2 Online teaching resources used by teachers

A research on college teacher's original teaching resource is also made among the participants of the study. It is illustrated in Figure 5. 3 that Chinese college teachers create more original text resources (71. 13%), while video, text, E-book, and 3D animation are evenly created by American college teachers and even some Apps are developed to assist teaching.

As for the quality of the various teaching resources, Chinese students and teachers (23. 43%) are more satisfied than American students and teachers (16. 49%). As shown in Figure 5. 4 and Figure 5. 5, more American students (9. 76%) and teachers (54. 27%) express dissatisfied with the quality of the

	Video	Audio	Text (including PPT)	App	Website	E-book	3D Animation
■ Chinese Teachers	14.20%	0	71.13%	0	0	13.57%	1.10%
■ American Teachers	30.56%	0	26.64%	0.79%	0	21.34%	20.67%

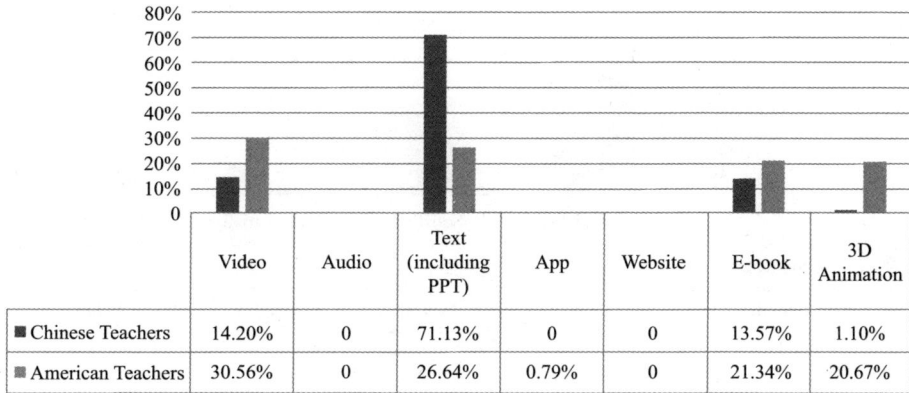

Figure 5. 3 Teaching resources created by teachers

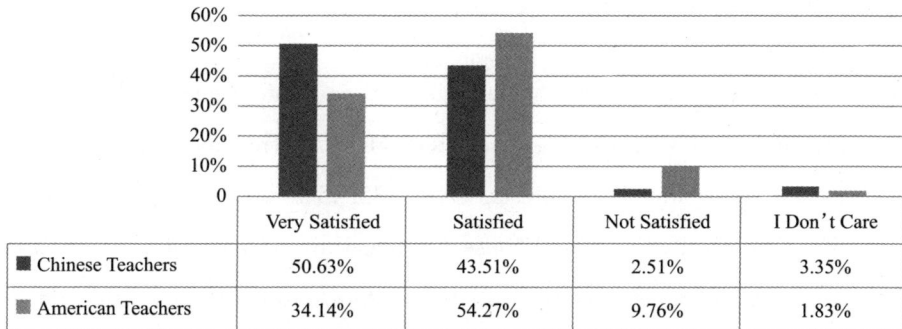

	Very Satisfied	Satisfied	Not Satisfied	I Don't Care
■ Chinese Teachers	50.63%	43.51%	2.51%	3.35%
■ American Teachers	34.14%	54.27%	9.76%	1.83%

Figure 5. 4 Teacher's satisfaction with teaching resources

teaching resources they are using. Through interview, we find that the reason lies in large amount of repetition, monotony in forms, and unattractive content.

It is also worthwhile to notice that more Chinese students and teacher do not care about the quality of online teaching resources. Also in the interview, it is found that the students study in a more passive way, that is, just following the teacher's guide, no active feedback. Comparingly, American students show great

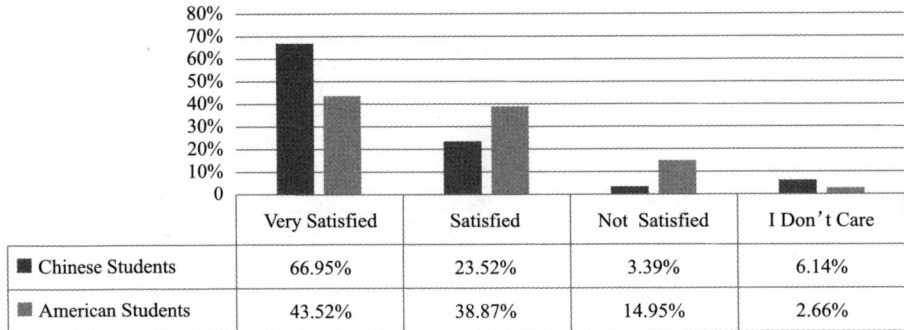

	Very Satisfied	Satisfied	Not Satisfied	I Don't Care
■ Chinese Students	66.95%	23.52%	3.39%	6.14%
■ American Students	43.52%	38.87%	14.95%	2.66%

Figure 5. 5 Student's satisfaction with teaching resources

attention, participation, and activity in online teaching.

5. 3. 3 Platform and technology

Most Chinese college use the following online platforms to teach: Chaoxing、Xuexitong, ICVE, Chinese University MOOC, Treenity, etc. Of all the colleges and universities in the present study, 35. 45% use Chaoxing and Xuexitong, 22. 23% use ICVE, 36. 12% use Chinese University MOOC, 3. 15% use Treenity, and 3. 05% use other educational platforms. In the United States, Moodle (58. 65%), Canvas (32. 61%)、Blackboard (8. 74%) are the top three platforms used in the researched colleges and universities. Meanwhile, Ding Talk and Tecent Meeting are the two mostly used platforms for real-time teaching, and the majority of American colleges use Zoom.

The two groups of teachers in the study show some similarities in grasping informational technology. More than 65% of them in both countries are capable to grasp and apply information technology in their online teaching. However both of the groups have over 18% teachers who can not use information technology proficiently in their teaching. Of them, the percentage of teachers over 45 years old are respectively 77. 58% in China and 80. 73% in America (Figure 5. 6).

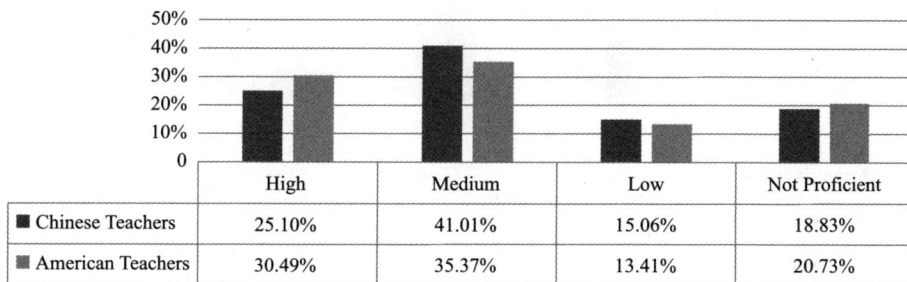

	High	Medium	Low	Not Proficient
■ Chinese Teachers	25.10%	41.01%	15.06%	18.83%
■ American Teachers	30.49%	35.37%	13.41%	20.73%

Figure 5. 6 Teachers' proficiency of information technology

In the research of problems met in their online teaching, low quality of image or voice, slow upload or download, lack of interactive function are ranked top three. In the interview of the teachers, both groups indicate that they suffered most difficulty in controlling the class processing and students' behaviors. Meanwhile system crash has ever happened in both countries, especially in the preliminary stage of the virus.

5. 3. 4 Satisfaction to the teaching effectiveness

Generally speaking, Chinese students show higher satisfaction to online teaching compared with American students (Figure 5. 7). "Very satisfied" Chinese students are 8% more America, while "Satisfied " American students are slightly competitive. In the teachers research (Figure 5. 8), Chinese teachers show great advantage in both "Very satisfied" and "Satisfied" items. Accordingly, American students and teachers think their online teaching "Ok" or "Dissatisfied" .

	Very Satisfied	Satisfied	Not Satisfied	I Don't Care
■ Chinese Students	23.09%	56.36%	12.92%	7.63%
■ American Students	15.61%	60.47%	7.97%	15.95%

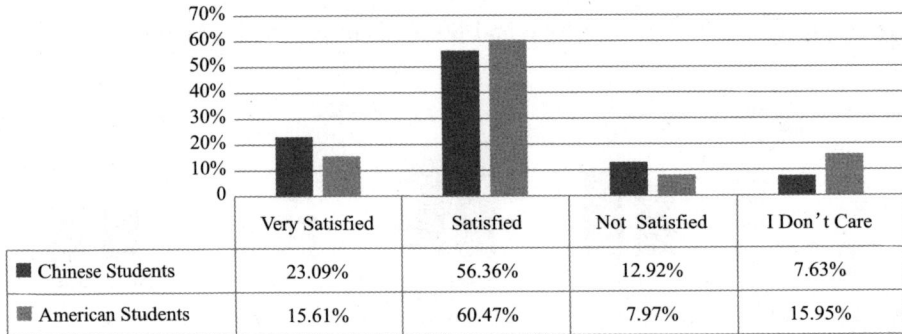

Figure 5. 7 Students' satisfaction with online teaching

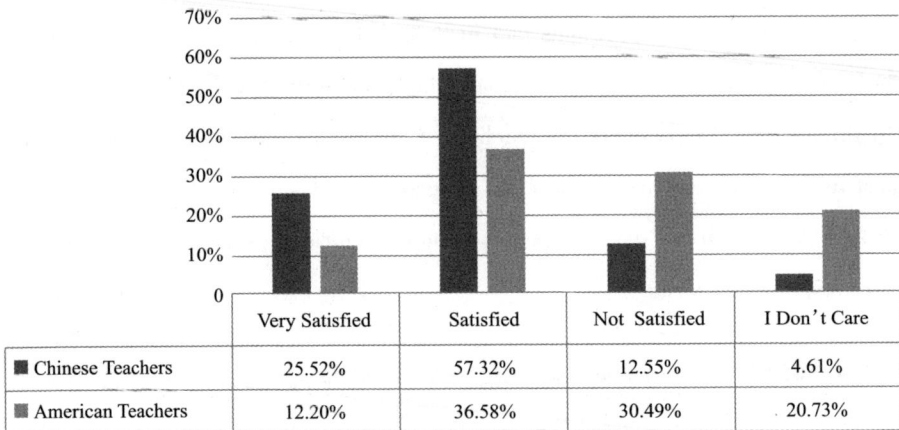

	Very Satisfied	Satisfied	Not Satisfied	I Don't Care
■ Chinese Teachers	25.52%	57.32%	12.55%	4.61%
■ American Teachers	12.20%	36.58%	30.49%	20.73%

Figure 5. 8 Teachers' satisfaction with online teaching

We also find in the interview that most Chinese students are most satisfied with the relaxed teaching atmosphere and dissatisfied with the poor quality of online resources. To American students, the interesting teaching style is most welcomed, but large amount of self-study assignments are most complained. Seemingly, most Chinese teachers are satisfied with the various kinds of teaching resources, and dissatisfied with the difficulty in controlling the class. Considering the sudden breakout of the virus, most American teachers think they are not very prepared for the online teaching. So they feel appreciate to the cooperation and coordination between teachers and students in fulfilling the teaching task. Similar to Chinese teachers, uncontrol of the class and students is also reflected by the American teachers.

5. 4 Problems in the online teaching of Chinese colleges

Online teaching has developed more than for 20 years in China. Series of achievements have arrived, from excellent courses, MOOC, to excellent shared courses. The form, resource, technology, and effectiveness of online education are warmly welcomed by college teachers and students. However by comparing with American colleges, several problems are worth our awareness and attention.

5. 4. 1 Not forming the habit of online teaching and learning

Although information and internet technology have been used in more and more educational areas and the blending teaching mode has become a new hotspot in academic research, many college teachers' online teaching is refined to playing PowerPoint, video, and pictures and only such functions of teaching platform as correcting homework and test are used. The students in the online class just watch the resources uploaded by the teachers, do the assignments and upload, and take a test. The interactive real – time teaching seldom happens. Therefore, it is of high importance to form the habit of using real – time online teaching in daily teaching. On the one hand, students can make the best use of their off – line time to learn whatever they are interested in and compensate for their online learning. It helps to satisfy their different specific requirement of learning. On the other hand, the teachers and students are more prepared and qualified to deal with the teaching in crucial period.

5. 4. 2 The practicability of course resource need to be enhanced

In 2003, the National Department of Education published a document *Initiation on constructing excellent online courses in higher education*. In 2010, Shandong Vocational College of Light Industry constructed the first excellent course on a provincial scale. Till now, more than 200 excellent courses, 50 excellent resources shared courses, and 150 online courses have been completed. Online courses have covered 80% of course catalogues in different fields. However, the problem of low practicability is highlighted in the study. It comes from the low quality of the teaching resources. From the result of the questionnaire, we can find text and PowerPoint cover the absolute majority among different kinds of resources. It cannot attract students' attention and support teachers' teaching effectively. It is also true to some courses developed long time, like College English, which was established in the year of 2018, and has 118 videos, 89 texts, and 106 audio resources. Besides, teachers find some videos and audios are too long to keep holding students' attention in class. Besides it is challenging for the teaching to control students' class behaviors and feedback. To some extent, that explains why more than 5% of Chinese students don't care for the quality of online teaching resources.

5. 4. 3 Similar functions and lacking of characteristics

Many college teachers were not clear about the different functions, methods, and characteristics. As a result, they changed teaching platform and method frequently to assist their class, which caused certain negative effects to their students. Based on a thorough analysis of the various teaching platforms, the major functions are focused on such online activities: resource upload and download, sign-in, test, evaluation, result analysis, questionnaires, etc. Therefore the relationship between technology and teaching is not targeted and pertinent. The support that online teaching platforms provide to college teachers is very limited.

5. 4. 4 Informational competence to be promoted

It is predicted from the study that college teachers' age is in an inverse proportion to the degree of information technology grasp. Especially to teachers over 45 years old, the status of information technology competence is negative in both countries. The traditional teaching mode has a stronger effect on the senior teachers, which causes the slow transfer of knowledge and technology. It will take a long time for them to accept and adapt to the new teaching atmosphere. Therefore information teaching technology should be popularized mainly in the senior teachers' group.

5. 4. 5 Lacking research on online teaching

Teaching and research coordinate each other. Researches on online course construction, teaching resource development, and blended-teaching mode have obtained their results, which helped us complete the teaching during the crucial period. In the interview of our study, we find that research activities on online teaching are seldom carried out in colleges of Shandong Province. In Mississippi

College, Lunch and Learn are organized regularly to provide teachers an opportunity to communicate the issues or problems in their teaching. Every time, a teacher presents on a certain topic he or she interests, then the listeners will have a heated discussion based on their teaching experience, sometimes even Brainstorming. Online teaching is covered in this activity repeatedly. A lot of teaching resources, such as Apps and platforms, are introduced in detail and shared among teachers of various fields. In addition, teachers learn to improve their information competence effectively by helping one another. So research activities on online teaching are of high importance in developing online education and teachers' information competence.

5.5 Strategies in online education development

5.5.1 Forming the habit of online teaching and learning by application of recorded teaching and live teaching

College teachers should combine recorded teaching and live teaching online in their daily practice. It is the key that the choice of teaching channels should be based on the characteristics of different courses. Generally speaking, there are two rules to follow. The literature—related course will be better elaborated by live teaching online. Supposing the students just watch a video about a passage on art or history, the knowledge may be delivered and understood, but it's very difficult to evoke students' sympathy for the common issues. Therefore the students will have a better understanding and sense of the content and context through real—time communication with the teachers in class. If the class is full of operations, like the courses in the mechanical category, recorded teaching can be preferred. By watching the videos on iPad or laptop, the students can follow the procedure step by step in detail. The video can be played repeatedly, fasted backward or forward till they grasp the techniques. In addition, some elective courses, especially the appreciation and criticism ones, can also be taught by combing the two ways. Recorded teaching is used in prevision and revision of the class by the students. Based on this, the live teaching online will be more effective and profound. In all, practicing using different ways in daily teaching will help us to form the habit of online teaching and learning, hence well prepared us for the emergency of the teaching environment.

5. 5. 2 Upgrade the function of teaching resources and platforms by deleting, revising, and constructing

We should calm down to classify and upgrade the present teaching resources instead of pursuing the quantity. Based on the features of the courses and learners, we can upgrade the present online course in three steps. First, deleting. That is, delete the inapplicable resources that do not attract students' interest. Second, improving. We should use information technology to enhance the quality of the resources that have good teaching content, but are not demonstrated in a appealing way. Third, updating. With the development of different industries, more and more techniques, materials, and cases are to be added to our present teaching content, particularly in vocational education. Therefore, the online teaching repositories should be updated to meet the development of different industries.

College teachers should qualify ourselves to conform to the new trend and construct novel teaching resources. First of all, we should recognize the functions, advantages and disadvantages of different online platforms. It lays a solid foundation for smart selections in our teaching. The purpose of online teaching will be more effective, instead of just using internet technology. Then, in the evaluation system of online class, such objective criteria as usage rate should be weakened, which helps teachers to construct and use online class according to their real needs in teaching. In addition, the internet technology companies should know more requirements of online teaching, and serve college teachers better by developing more functional, practical, and effective teaching platforms and resources.

5.5.3 Improving college teachers' informational qualification by competition, training, and daily practice

At present, two channels are normally used to improve college teachers' informational qualification. One is collective training in winter vacation or summer vacation. This kind of training usually has a specific topic and trainees have enough time to participate in the learning activities. However, lacking of the application in real teaching is a kind of a shortcoming. After all, the best way to understand and grasp a method or technique is to use it in real teaching. Only by practice, making mistakes, and correction, can the method or technique be turned into our competence. The other way is to train by competition. Nowadays, various teaching contests are organized to motivate teachers' application of online teaching. It encourages teachers to design and create their classes in an updated way. And it is the best that information technology is really applied to teaching. Teaching and technology are perfectly combined in the contest. Nevertheless, most of the competitors are comparatively young, good-looking, and speak standard language, which are the guarantee for win. The result is only a small a mount of teachers have the opportunity to improve themselves by joining contests. So the two ways should be connected to train college teachers' information competence. The choice of training method can be based on the characteristics of trainees. Particularly for teachers over 45 years old, training schedules should be designed according to their characteristics in age, psychology, knowledge, mentality, etc. Only in this way can we construct the atmosphere of online teaching and improve the informational competence of college teachers overall.

5. 5. 4 Encourage online teaching research by transforming research achievements

Colleges, companies and teachers should be united to form research groups and strive to make breakthrough in the study of online teaching. Each party takes responsibility. The colleges make positive policies to support the research. The companies provide technological support. And college teachers take an active part in the projects. Such hotproblems as improving the quality of online teaching resources, evaluation of online teaching result, improving teaching information competence, etc. should be highlighted in the research. Meanwhile, we should pay attention to collecting the achievements arrived in the research, and transform them into papers, patents, books, etc. It would motivate the implementation of online teaching research and serve teachers' promotion in their careers.

Ending

The development of foreign language teaching activities in colleges and universities is not only the explanation and introduction of language but also the explanation and teaching of culture. In the practice of learning, we can establish the teaching idea of "culture first", form comprehensive teaching content and apply a three – dimensional linkage teaching method, build a complementary teaching team to carry out cross – cultural ability training activities in four aspects, deepen students' perception and understanding of Chinese culture, improve the international ability, strengthen cultural confidence in the enhancement of cultural identity, and train qualified builders and reliable successors of socialism with Chinese characteristics.

Information technology is a big impetus for intercultural foreign language teaching. The online and offline teaching resources involve the learners in a real intercultural environment and enable them to practise communication skills more efficiently and pleasantly. Their learning will not be limited in a classroom at a certain time. Foreign language learning and teaching are extended to any time and space.

All in all, technology helps to build a learner–friendly teaching mode which improves the application of intercultural approach to foreign language teaching. With the development of information technology, more and more teachers will benefit from intercultural approach not only in teaching foreign languages but also in mother tongues.

Appendix

跨文化交际能力调查

目的：下列问题是用于测试您的跨文化交际能力，请注意：

·如实选择；

·您的回答将被保密；

·这不是考试，并没有回答正确和错误之分。

提示：下列问题是在生活和学习场景中中国人与外国人交际时的描述，题目中的"外国人""外国教授""外国朋友""外籍教师"等的"外国""外籍"均指**西方英语国家**。请根据实际情况进行选择。

基本情况

1. 年龄：18~25 岁□　　25~35 岁□　　35 岁以上□

2. 性别：男□　　女□

3. 受教育程度：本科□　　硕士研究生□　　博士研究生□

4. 专业：英语□　　非英语□

5. 你学习英语几年了？

6. 你的英文水平：交流有困难□　　能够应付日常会话□　　交流无障碍□

7. 你是否修过跨文化交际方面的课程？是□　　否□

8. 你平时是否有较多的机会和外国人接触？是□　　否□

9. 你是否知道在与西方人交流时哪些问题可以问，哪些不可以问？

是□ 否□

10. 您在与西方人交流时是否知道手势语等非语言行为也会导致误解或产生沟通障碍？是□ 否□

11. 你能列举出西方人的一些文化禁忌吗？

测试内容

1. 你对西方人的基本交际方式风格了解程度如何？

A. 非常了解　　　　　　　　B. 有一定了解

C. 不太了解　　　　　　　　D. 基本不了解

2. 我知道相同的手势在不同的文化中可能含义不同，所以在交际中我会有意识地避免使用会引起误解的手势。

A. 一直这样做　　　　　　　B. 有时这样做

C. 很少这样做　　　　　　　D. 从未这样做

3. 中、西方人交际时的冲突根源在于文化差异。

A. 完全同意　　　　　　　　B. 基本同意

C. 不太同意　　　　　　　　D. 完全不同意

4. 与西方人交谈时，若想拒绝别人的请求，我通常会通过言外之意让对方体会到。

A. 一向如此　　　　　　　　B. 多数时候

C. 比较少　　　　　　　　　D. 从不

5. 与外国人交流时，我常常会误解他们的意思。

A. 一向如此　　　　　　　　B. 多数时候

C. 比较少　　　　　　　　　D. 从不

6. 我通常能理解外国人的一些非语言行为（如手势、面部表情等）所表达的含义。

A. 一向如此　　　　　　　　B. 多数时候

C. 比较少   D. 从不

7. 在外国教授的讲座中，如果我对他的观点有异议，我不会直接指出。

A. 一向如此   B. 多数时候

C. 比较少   D. 从不

8. 为了保持和谐的关系，我会避免与外国朋友在一些意见上产生冲突。

A. 一向如此   B. 多数时候

C. 比较少   D. 从不

9. 你认为避免冲突是尊敬他人的体现吗？

A. 完全同意   B. 基本同意

C. 不太同意   D. 不同意

10. 如果你有一个很好的想法，但担心可能不会被对方（指外国朋友、老板或外教）接受，你会提出来吗？

A. 一定会   B. 可能会

C. 可能不会   D. 一定不会

11. 来自异国的人否认了我的想法，我会感到沮丧。

A. 完全同意   B. 基本同意

C. 不太同意   D. 不同意

12. 西方人高度赞赏个人成就并将此作为成功的标志。对于这样的做法，你怎么看？

A. 赞同   B. 基本赞同

C. 不确定   D. 难以接受

13. 你是否理解外国人自我的、不参考他人意见的作决定风格？

A. 完全理解   B. 基本理解

C. 不太理解   D. 难以理解

14. 在课堂上，外籍教师当众否定了我的提议，我会觉得很没面子。

A. 完全同意   B. 基本同意

C. 不太同意   D. 不同意

15. 假如现在你有一份收入稳定的工作，但提升机会渺茫，而另有一份低收入却有较多发展机会的工作，你会跳槽吗？

A. 一定会   B. 可能会

C. 不太会   D. 不会

16. 你是否意识到不同文化对异类思想的接纳程度有所不同？

A. 完全意识到   B. 有点意识到

C. 没有意识到   D. 没有注意过

17. 如果在工作中你要展开一项新的行动，你会在有多大把握的时候决定去做？

A. 90%以上   B. 70%以上

C. 50%以上   D. 30%以上

18. 我了解中、西方人对"平等"持不同的看法。

A. 完全了解   B. 基本了解

C. 不太了解   D. 不了解

19. 在外教课上，外籍教师以学生为中心的、以讨论为主讲解为辅的教学方法可能一时让你难以适应，你会觉得____。

A. 完全可以接受   B. 不习惯，但可以接受

C. 不太能接受   D. 不能接受

20. 如果外教交给你一项任务，但你觉得他的计划不太好，你仍然会遵循他的计划展开工作吗？

A. 一定会   B. 基本会

C. 不太会   D. 不会

21. 在按外教的计划展开工作时，如果你发现有更好的方法完成任

务，你会改动外教的计划吗？

    A. 一定会   B. 基本会

    C. 不太会   D. 不会

22. 你能接受一位女性作你团队的领导吗？

    A. 完全可以   B. 基本可以

    C. 不太能接受   D. 不能接受

23. 当你回答"我会马上去做"，你指的"马上"是____。

    A. 立刻   B. 今天之内

    C. 两三天   D. 一个星期之内

24. 假设某天你到外教办公室请教一个问题，发现外教正在与他人交谈。你在一旁想等待时机进行提问，但外教请你另约时间。对这样的做法，你觉得____。

    A. 合情合理   B. 无所谓

    C. 不礼貌

25. 我外语流利，但与外国人交流时还是会感到紧张和害怕。

    A. 一向如此   B. 多数时候

    C. 比较少   D. 从不

26. 中国文化优于外国文化，对这样的看法，你____。

    A. 完全同意   B. 基本同意

    C. 不太同意   D. 不同意

27. 我愿意与外国人交流，但不知道如何与他们交流才能避免误会。

    A. 完全同意   B. 基本同意

    C. 不太同意   D. 不同意

28. 我对外国朋友的文化和语言感到好奇，我愿意学习对方文化方面的知识。

    A. 完全同意   B. 基本同意

C. 不太同意 D. 不同意

29. 当你同外国朋友发生冲突的时候，你会设法从他的文化角度考虑问题吗？

A. 一向如此 B. 多数时候

C. 比较少 D. 从不

30. 如果你要出国学习深造，面对完全陌生的语言文化环境，你会感到焦虑和担心吗？

A. 会 B. 可能会

C. 不太会 D. 不会

31. 我喜欢并欣赏外国人常常直接提出自己不同观点的做法。

A. 完全同意 B. 基本同意

C. 不太同意 D. 不同意

32. 假如你进入公司实习，要与外商进行谈判，在此之前你会先请他们吃饭或带他们观光以建立一个和谐的关系吗？

A. 肯定会 B. 可能会

C. 不太会 D. 不会

33. 与外国朋友交际中，对于没有听懂的地方，我常常会____。

A. 装作听懂了 B. 不知道该怎样处理

C. 请对方解释

34. 对于那些不符合中国文化的行为，如外国人见面施亲吻礼，我感到____。

A. 不能接受 B. 能接受，但不愿意做

C. 能接受，也愿意做

35. 和外国人交谈时，我善于观察他们不同于中国的交际方式（如美国人说话比较直接明了；日本人则喜欢保持沉默）。

A. 一向如此 B. 多数时候

C. 比较少　　　　　　　　　　D. 从不

36. 我认为给对方留面子是重要的交际规则，无论中国人还是外国人都应该遵守。

A. 完全同意　　　　　　　　　B. 基本同意

C. 不太同意　　　　　　　　　D. 不同意

37. 一旦发现对方不同的交际风格，我会注意调整自己的交际行为。

A. 一向如此　　　　　　　　　B. 多数时候

C. 比较少　　　　　　　　　　D. 从不

38. 你是否经常在讲英语的同时不自觉地用中国人的手势语？

A. 一向如此　　　　　　　　　B. 多数时候

C. 比较少　　　　　　　　　　D. 从不

39. 我会对本国文化和异国文化知识进行比较，了解异同。

A. 一向如此　　　　　　　　　B. 多数时候

C. 比较少　　　　　　　　　　D. 从不

Bibliography

[1] Aarup Jensin A. Defining Intercultural Competence for the Adult Learner [M]//Aarup Jensin A, Jæger K, Lorentsen A. Intercultural Competence: A New Challenge for Language Teachers and Trainers in Europe (Volum Ⅱ: The Adult Learner). Aalborg: Aalborg University Press, 1995.

[2] Allen D E, Valette R M. Classroom techniques: Foreign Language and English as a Second Language [M]. New York: Harcourt Brace Jovanovich Inc., 1977.

[3] Anthony E M. Approach, method and technique [J]. English Language Teaching, 1963, 17: 63-67.

[4] Arasaratnam L A. Intercultural Communication Competence from Multiple Cultural Perspectives: A new Theoretical Model and Empirical Validation [D]. USA: Graduate School-New Brunswick Rutgers, State University of New Jersey, 2003.

[5] Binon J, Claes M T. Intercultural Communication and Negotiation in a Business Environment [M] //Aarup Jensin A, Jæger K, Lorentsen A. Intercultural Competence: A New Challenge for Language Teachers and Trainers in Europe (Volum Ⅱ: The Adult Learner). Aalborg: Aalborg University Press, 1995.

[6] Bredella L. For a Flexible Model of Intercultural Understanding [M]//余

卫华. 跨文化研究读本. 武汉：武汉大学出版社，2006.

［7］ Byram M. Teaching Culture and Language：Towards an Integrated Model ［M］//Buttjes D，Byram M. Mediating Language and Cultures. Cleve-don：Multilingual Matters，1991.

［8］ Byram M. Intercultural Foreign Language Learning and Teaching ［M］// Aarup Jensin A，Jæger K，Lorentsen A. Intercultural Competence：A New Challenge for Language Teachers and Trainers in Europe（Volum Ⅱ：The Adult Learner）. Aalborg：Aalborg University Press，1995.

［9］ Byram M. Assessing intercultural competence in language teaching ［J］. Sprogforum，2000，18（6）：8-13.

［10］ Canale M，Swain M. Theoretical Bases of Communicative Approaches to Second Language Teaching and Testing ［M］//桂诗春. Applied Linguistics 1. 湖南：湖南教育出版社，1987.

［11］ Canale M. From Communicative Competence to Communicative Language Pedagogy ［M］//Richards J C，Schmidt R W. Language and Communication. London：Longman Book，1983.

［12］ Chen G M. Relationships of the dimensions of intercultural communication competence ［J］. Communication Quarterly，1989，37：118-133.

［13］ Chen G M. Intercultural communication competence：some perspectives of research ［J］. The Howard Journal of Communication，1990，2（3）：243-261.

［14］ Chen G M. A Test of intercultural communication competence ［J］. Intercultural Communication Studies Ⅱ，1992，2：63-82.

［15］ Chen G M，Starosta W J. Foundations of Intercultural Communication ［M］. USA：A Viacom Company，1998.

［16］ Chen G M. A model of global communication competence ［J］. China

Media Research, 2005, 1 (1): 3-11.

[17] Chomsky. Aspects of the Theory of Syntax [M]. Cambridge, Mass: MIT Press, 1965.

[18] Cunningsworth A. Choosing Your Coursebook [M]. Shanghai: Shanghai Foreign Language Education Press, 2002.

[19] Dodd C H. Dynamics of Intercultural Communication [M]. 5th ed. Shanghai: Shanghai Foreign Language Education Press, 2006.

[20] Dubin F, Olshtain E. Course Design [M]. Shanghai: Shanghai Foreign Language Education Press, 2002.

[21] Fantini A E. A Central Concern: Developing Intercultural Competence (Adapted from A Report by the Intercultural Communicative Competence Task Force) [M] //World Learning. USA: Brattleboro, VT, 1994.

[22] Gertsen M C. Intercultural Training as In-Service Training: A Discussion of Possible Approaches [M]//Aarup Jensin A, Jæger K, Lorentsen A. Intercultural Competence: A New Challenge for Language Teachers and Trainers in Europe (Volum Ⅱ: The Adult Learner). Aalborg: Aalborg University Press, 1995.

[23] Gudykunst W B. Being Perceived as a Competence Communicator [M]//Gudykunst W B, Kim Y Y. Reading on Communicating Strangers. New York: McGraw-Hill, 1992.

[24] Hymes D. On Communicative Competence [M]//John B. Pride, Janet Holmes. Sociolinguistics. Harmondsworth: Penguin, 1972.

[25] Jæger K. Teaching Intercultural Competence to University Students [M]//Aarup Jensin A, Jæger K, Lorentsen A. Intercultural Competence: A New Challenge for Language Teachers and Trainers in Europe (Volum Ⅱ: The Adult Learner). Denmark: Aalborg University,

1995.

[26] Jeremy H. The Practice of English Language Teaching [M]. London and New York: Longman Publishing, 1991.

[27] Kaplan R B. Cultural Thought Patterns [J]. Intercultural Education Language Learning, 1996, 16: 1-20.

[28] Kim Y Y. Intercultural Communication Competence: A Systems-Theoretic View [M]//Toomey S T, Korzenny R. Cross-cultural Interpersonal Communication. Newbury Park, CA: Sage, 1991.

[29] Kim Y Y. Becoming Intercultural: An Integrative Theory of Communication and Cross-cultural Adaptation [M]. Thousand Oaks, California: Sage Publications Inc. , 2001.

[30] Kobrin S. International Expertise in American Business [M]. New York: Institute of International Education, 1984.

[31] Kroeber A L, Kluckhohohn C. Culture: A critical review of concepts and definitions [J]. Harvard University Peabody Museum of American Archaeology and Ethnology Papers, 1952 (47): 181.

[32] Littlewood W. Communicative Language Teaching [M]. Cambridge: Cambridge University Press, 1981.

[33] Lustig M W, Koester J. Intercultural Competence: Interpersonal Communication Cross Cultures [M]. 3rd ed. New York: Addison Wesley Longman Inc. , 1999.

[34] Marsella A J. The measurement of emotional reactions to work: Methodological and research issues [J]. Work and Stress, 1994 (8): 166-167.

[35] McLuhan M. Understanding Media [M]. New York: Mentor,1964.

[36] Meyer M. Developing Transcultural Competence: Case Studies of Ad-

vanced Language Learners [M]//Buttjes D, Byram M. Mediating Languages and Cultures: Towards an Intercultural Theory of Foreign Language Education. Clevedon, UK: Multilingual Matters, 1991.

[37] Müller Bernd-Dietrich. An Intercultural Theory of Teaching German as a Foreign Language [M]//Aarup Jensin A, Jæge, K, Lorentsen A. Intercultural Competence: A New Challenge for Language Teachers and Trainers in Europe (Volum II: The Adult Learner). Aalborg: Aalborg University Press, 1995.

[38] Nolan R W. Communicating and Adapting Across Cultures: Living and Working in the Global Village [M]. Westport: Greenwood Publishing Group, 1999.

[39] Ovando C J, Collier V P. Bilingual and ESL Classroom: Teaching in Multicultural Contexts [M]. McGraw-Hill Book Co. , 1985.

[40] PaigeR M. Cultural competency training: Developing intercultural skills for diversity [J]. An Intercultural Leadership Workshop for Intermediated School District, 2003, 4 (10): 287.

[41] Paulston C B, Brude M N. Teaching English as a Second Language: Techniques and Procedures [M]. Cambridge Massachusettrs: Winthrop Publishers, INC, 1976.

[42] Picht R. Foreign languages and international studies: A plea for greater Europcan cooperation [J]. European Journal of Education, 1983, 18 (2).

[43] Revell J. Teaching Techniques for Communicative English [M]. Macmillan Publishers Ltd. , 1983.

[44] Richards J C, Rodgers T S. Approaches and Methods in Language Teaching [M]. Foreign Language Teaching and Research Press & Cam-

bridge University Press, 2000.

[45] Ruben B D. Assessing communication competency for intercultural adaptation [J]. Group and Organization Studies, 1976, 1: 334-354.

[46] Samovar L A, Porter R E. Communication Between Cultures [M]. 5th ed. Beijing: Peking University Press, 2004.

[47] Spitzberg B H, Cupach W. Interpersonal Communication Competence [M]. Beverly Hill, CA: Sage, 1984.

[48] Spitzberg B H. Communication Competence: Measures of Perceived Effectiveness [M]//Charles H Tardy. A Handbook for the Study of Human Communication. Norwood. NJ: Ablex, 1988.

[49] Stern H H. Fundamental Concepts of Language Teaching [M]. Shanghai: Shanghai Foreign Language Teaching Press, 2000.

[50] Tylor E B. Primitive Culture [M]. London: John Murray, 1871.

[51] Wiemann J M, Backlund P. Current theory and research in communicative competence [J]. Review of Educational Research, 1980, 50: 185-199.

[52] Whorf B L. The Relation of Habitual Thought and Behavior to Language [M]//Carroll J B. Language, Thought, and Reality. Cambridge, MA: MIT Press, 1956.

[53] 毕继万. 谈跨文化交际中的"能力"[R]. 南京: 第六届跨文化交际研究会年会, 2005.

[54] 陈建平. 案例教学法与商务英语教学 [J]. 宁波大学学报(教育科学版), 2004 (5): 113-115.

[55] 陈俊森, 樊葳葳, 钟华. 跨文化交际与外语教学 [M]. 武汉: 华中科技大学出版社, 2006.

[56] 戴炜栋. 构建具有中国特色的英语教学"一条龙"体系 [J]. 外语

教学与研究，2001（5）：322-327.

［57］戴炜栋，任庆梅. 外语教学与教师专业发展：理论与实践［M］. 上海：上海外语教育出版社，2007.

［58］高耀. 在线教学需注意的五个问题［N］. 中国科学报，2020-03-31.

［59］高永晨. 大学生跨文化交际能力的现状调查和对策研究［J］. 外语与外语教学，2006（1）：26-55.

［60］胡文仲，高一虹. 外语教学与文化［M］. 长沙：湖南教育出版社，1997.

［61］胡文仲. 论跨文化交际的实证研究［J］. 外语教学与研究，2005（5）：323-327.

［62］胡文仲. 跨文化交际学概论［M］. 北京：外语教学与研究出版社，2006.

［63］黄文祥，李亚东，张喜生. 我国本科高校线上教学的质量状况、评价及建议［J］. 中国高等教育，2020（8）：4.

［64］贾玉新. 跨文化交际学［M］. 上海：上海外语教育出版社，2004.

［65］李萍，唐琪. 疫情期间在线教学得失几何：代表委员谈疫情影响下的在线教育：上［N］. 中国教育报，2020-05-26.

［66］刘齐生. "跨文化能力"之概念及其引出的问题［J］. 广东外语外贸大学学报，2004，15（4）：33-36.

［67］王振亚. 社会文化测试分析［C］//胡文仲. 文化与交际. 北京：外语教学与研究出版社，1994.

［68］文秋芳. 英语口语测试与教学［M］. 上海：上海外语教育出版社，1999.

［69］吴亚. 大学英语专业学生跨文化敏感度测评及研究［D］. 重庆：重庆大学，2006.

［70］徐锦芬. 现代外语教学的理论与实践［M］. 武汉：华中科技大学出

版社，2006.

[71] 许力生. 跨文化交流入门 [M]. 杭州：浙江大学出版社，2006.

[72] 杨盈，庄恩平. 构建外语教学跨文化交际能力框架 [J]. 外语界，2007（4）：13-21.

[73] 杨盈. 构建外语教学跨文化能力框架 [D]. 上海：上海大学，2007.

[74] 张红玲. 跨文化外语教学 [M]. 上海：上海外语教育出版社，2007.

[75] 赵爱国，姜雅明. 应用语言文化学概论 [M]. 上海：上海外语教育出版社，2003.

[76] 赵厚宪. 外语教学中的文化教学原则 [J]. 中国英语教学，2002（6）：52-53.

[77] 钟华，樊葳葳，秦傲松. 非英语专业学生社会文化能力调查 [J]. 外语界，2001（4）：19-34.

[78] 庄恩平. 经济全球化背景下跨文化交际学研究的思考 [J]. 中国外语，2006（1）：57-61.

[79] 高等学校英语专业英语教学大纲 [M]. 上海：上海外语教学与研究出版社，2000.